Kung-Fu

*The Ultimate Guide to Shaolin Kung Fu
Along with Its Movements and Techniques*

Contents

INTRODUCTION..1

CHAPTER 1: WHAT IS KUNG-FU? 3

    7 Kung-Fu Disciplines 8

CHAPTER 2: SHAOLIN KUNG FU VS. OTHER STYLES 16

    What Makes the Different Styles of Kung Fu Unique? 16

    Understanding Shaolin Kung Fu 17

    Philosophy of Shaolin Kung Fu 17

    Fighting Techniques and Methods of Shaolin Kung Fu 18

    Wing Chun 18

    Tai Chi 19

    Northern Praying Mantis 20

    Baguazhang 21

    Xing Yi Quan 22

    Bajiquan 23

    Benefits of Kung Fu Practice 24

    Which Kung Fu Style Should You Learn 24

    What is the Deadliest Kung Fu Style? 25

    Most Practical Kung Fu Style for Self Defense 25

    Kung Fu and the Modern World 25

THE POPULARITY OF KUNG FU STYLES IN WESTERN COUNTRIES 26

CHAPTER 3: THE 5 ANIMAL PATTERNS OF KUNG FU 28

TIGER 29

DRAGON 32

CRANE 35

SNAKE 37

LEOPARD 39

CHAPTER 4: STANCES IN KUNG FU 42

SIGNIFICANCE OF STANCES IN KUNG FU 42

HORSE STANCE 44

FORWARD STANCE 45

CAT STANCE 47

TWIST STANCE 49

CRANE STANCE 51

BOW STANCE 53

LOWER STANCE 53

CHAPTER 5: THE LOHAN PATTERN 55

ORIGIN OF THE LOHAN PATTERN 55

IMPORTANCE OF LOHAN HAND PATTERNS FOR KUNG FU 56

THE IMPORTANCE OF CHI KUNG FOR KUNG FU 57

PRACTICING THE LOHAN PATTERN 57

IMPORTANCE OF PRACTICING WITH A MASTER 58

THE BASICS OF THE LOHAN PATTERNS 58

PRACTICING THE LOHAN PATTERN EXERCISES 69

FINDING A KUNG FU MASTER TRAINER 70

LOHAN PATTERN EXERCISES FOR BEGINNERS 70

LOHAN PATTERN EXERCISES FOR WEIGHT LOSS 71

CHAPTER 6: CHI AND ZEN IN KUNG FU 72

UNDERSTANDING CHI 72

TYPES OF CHI 73

FEELING CHI 74

WORKING WITH CHI 75

CHI EXERCISES 76

CHI, QIGONG, AND SHAOLIN KUNG FU 78

UNDERSTANDING ZEN 79

ZEN AND SHAOLIN KUNG FU 79

FINDING AND MASTERING ZEN IN YOUR DAILY LIFE 81

CHAPTER 7: WEAPONS OF KUNG FU 84

CHAPTER 8: STRIKING AND LAMA PAI KUNG FU 93

STRIKING FUNDAMENTALS OF LAMA PAI 94

DIFFERENT STRIKING TECHNIQUES 94

LAMA PAI AND THE IMPORTANCE OF SELF-DEFENSE 100

THREE FORMS OR CATEGORIES OF LAMA PAI 101

CHAPTER 9: KICKING IN KUNG FU 104

THE CHARACTERISTICS OF A GOOD KICK 105

BASIC KICKS 106

ADVANCED KICKS 114

CHAPTER 10: SELF-DEFENSE IN KUNG FU 118

WING CHUN TODAY 119

FUNDAMENTALS OF SELF-DEFENSE 120

TECHNIQUES OF WING CHUN 122

CHAPTER 11: DAILY TRAINING DRILLS 125

STRETCHING 128

WARM-UP 129

COMBAT 130

STRIKING 131

KICKING 133

SELF-DEFENSE 134

GENERAL KUNG FU WORKOUT IDEAS 135

CONCLUSION 137

HERE'S ANOTHER BOOK BY CLINT SHARP THAT YOU
MIGHT LIKE..139

REFERENCES 140

Introduction

Most people's first introduction to martial arts was either through movies or TV shows. Strong, steadfast, disciplined heroes fight seemingly impossible odds with nothing more than their arms, hands, legs, and feet. These heroes are ambassadors. They introduced the art form to audiences outside of China and Hong Kong. You don't have to live in either of those places to learn Kung-Fu properly.

This book is your portal to the dojos and kwoons. From the comfort of your own home and working at your own pace, you too can perform the dazzling kicks and purposeful movements of Kung-Fu. Whether you're a novice or already have some training under your belt, this book is designed to not only further your knowledge of martial art but to enhance the positive ripples that learning it can spread into every facet of your life.

Kung-Fu is more than just learning how to throw punches and kicks. It is all about discipline. This martial art is a fantastic way to get in and stay in great physical shape. In today's hectic and often demanding world, it can be a fantastic outlet to relieve stress and anxiety. Sharpening your body sharpens your mind and improves concentration.

On your journey with this book, you can discover the self-confidence you may lack or bolster the one you already have. By learning Kung-Fu with this guide, you will be connected, if not physically, in spirit with all the practitioners who came before you. You will join an ancient community, all sharing the goals of learning self-defense and improving themselves.

Kung-Fu is an art that promotes self-expression. You can take the foundations and expand on them to form something uniquely your own. Like a painter, this book will provide you with the paint, the brushes, and the canvas. And it'll teach you how to paint while leaving the final product up to you.

Chapter 1: What Is Kung-Fu?

Before learning Kung-Fu, it is paramount to understand where it came from. To get the most out of this book's lessons and the martial art itself, obtaining a firm grasp on its history and origins is essential. These are the building blocks that the discipline is built on. Like those of a house, these foundations help keep the whole structure together and prevent it from falling apart.

There are several accepted definitions or translations of "Kung-Fu." Some interpret it as "work and effort." Others feel that the translation to "hard work of a man" is more accurate. Whatever your interpretation, there are always two elements: hard work and dedication. Mastering martial art requires both.

The origins of Kung-Fu are disputed. With a country as old and as rich in history as China, narrowing it down to a single source is seemingly impossible. That said, there are mythological and historical breadcrumbs that you can follow to establish a rough timeline of the martial arts' origin.

Many believe the beginnings of what would eventually become Kung-Fu started with the introduction and spread of martial arts through China. Later known as "The Yellow Emperor," Huangdi was thought to have written some of the first guides on military tactics and self-defense techniques that would evolve into a fighting discipline.

According to legends, the stars foretold the Yellow Emperor's birth and great destiny. Born into a time of great strife and warring tribes, Huangdi would unite the different tribes that lived along the Yellow River. Unified, these groups became the first version of the Chinese State.

The Yellow Emperor not only influenced the political and military landscape of China, but he also was the forefather of Chinese medicine. His philosophies and medical discoveries would later evolve into some of the central tenets of Kung-Fu. Those writings are some of the oldest ever discovered in the history of mankind.

After the legendary Yellow Emperor passed away, his martial arts teachings continued and were built upon. Centuries of small-scale warfare between feudal lords over everything from land rights to personal affronts enveloped a still young China. In this phase, Huangdi's philosophies on martial arts, warfare, and self-improvement were adopted and adapted by different regions of the vast country.

The Yellow Emperor's philosophies evolved into Ancient China's "Six Arts." Extremely similar to the western concept of a "renaissance man," Chinese men, especially those in the upper class, we're encouraged to learn. These Six Arts were: archery, calligraphy, chariot riding, music, mathematics, music, and rites.

During the Han Dynasty, another influential figure in the development of Chinese martial arts came to the forefront of the movement. He was an infamous physician and surgeon named "Hua Tuo." Besides being credited with discovering anesthesia, the well-known doctor filled in the gaps regarding medicine in The Yellow Emperor's teachings.

Another gigantic contribution from Hua Tuo to Kung-Fu was the development of exercise techniques that had numerous health benefits for his patients. These techniques were based on animals he'd observed. He developed a system that would later be used in Shaolin-born Kung-Fu techniques using those movements he observed.

More centuries passed with various fighting styles, techniques, and life philosophies cultivated in mainland China. It wasn't until a foreign Buddhist monk from Southern India, Bodhidharma, visited the country that Kung-Fu was formed.

Bodhidharma came to mainland China sometime between 450-500 A.D. The details of how he got there and his travels across the country are unclear. There aren't a lot of records of his travels. What is known is that he originally came to teach and spread the word of what would become known as Xiao Sheng Buddhism.

The arrival of Bodhidharma was heralded by Indian royalty, requesting that the Kingdoms of China take good care of their monk who came to spread the teachings of Buddha. Wherever he went, the Chinese were eager to see him, hear him speak, and learn from him. But they were surprised when instead of speaking, he simply meditated. Some were intrigued, others confused, and there were even those who were angered. Whatever their reaction, most of the Chinese populace he came across didn't fully understand what he was preaching. With that said, word of him and his radical teachings spread.

Eventually, tales of Da Mo (Bodhidharma), the Indian meditating monk, reached the ears of the ruler of China's Southern Kingdom, Emperor Wu. A devout Buddhist, the emperor, made a point to erect monuments, statues, and temples dedicated to the religion. So, when he heard of this Indian monk with a new take on what he loved, he had to meet him.

There's a famous story of the first interaction between Emperor Wu and Bodhidharma. The Emperor inquired whether or not the monk thought that the leader's dedication to Buddhism and generous donations to the religious institutions were good and moral. To his surprise, the monk said "no." When he asked if a Buddha was living in their world, again, the monk said "no."

It probably goes without saying, but Bodhidharma's answers upset Emperor Wu. Their reasoning was simple and demonstrated how the monk saw the world and what he promoted through his teachings. Emperor Wu's grand donations to temples and Buddhist institutions weren't something to brag about or be proud of. As the monk saw it, this was a leader's duty. Even asking if a Buddha was living among them displayed a clear lack of faith in the religion. Bodhidharma was ordered to leave the kingdom and never return.

After his exile from Emperor Wu's kingdom, Bodhidharma's trip up to the Northern Part of China brought him to a gathering in the village of Nanjing. There, he came across a former prolific general named "Sheng Guang." Guilt over all the people he'd killed, directly or indirectly, and the effects that had on his victims' friends and families led him to become a Buddhist Monk.

On this day in Nanjing, Sheng Guang addressed a crowd of villagers, teaching them traditional Buddhist lessons. Bodhidharma listened to him and reacted accordingly, whether he agreed with what was being said or didn't. The fact that this foreigner would have the nerve to shake his head and not agree with his lessons angered Sheng Guang. That anger boiled over to the point that the former general snatched the Buddhist beads from around the monk's neck and threw some of them at him, hitting him in the face, bloodying him, and knocking out a few teeth.

Naturally, Sheng Guang thought his angry outburst would produce a confrontation with the South Indian monk. Surprisingly, Bodhidharma simply smiled and walked away. This act of self-control and the ability to turn the other cheek profoundly impacted the former general. It also demonstrated a core tenant of Kung-Fu, discipline, control, and the ability to manage one's anger. This so profoundly impacted Sheng Guang that he followed Bodhidharma all the way to the Shaolin Temple.

Legend has it that when Bodhidharma reached the Shaolin Temple, he was greeted by enthusiastic monks who'd heard about him and his teachings. They were excited. But he just walked past all of them without saying a word or even acknowledging their presence. Instead, he made his way towards the back of the temple. Once there, he found a cave, sat down, and started meditating.

It is said that Bodhidharma sat in that cave, staring at a wall, not even the entrance, for nine whole years. Can you imagine that? Sitting in place for almost a decade without even muttering a single word? They said that his meditating and praying was so intense that his silhouette left a print on that wall.

The Shaolin monks were blown away by Bodhidharma's dedication and faith. They made and offered him a room there at the temple. Though he never said a word, the Indian monk got up after nine years and walked into a room that was offered to him. He sat down and meditated for another four years.

A mystic grew around Bodhidharma. His unorthodox teachings started to catch on with the Shaolin monks. They began to appreciate his approach to the religious teachings they'd dedicated their lives to. Though they weren't physically or spiritually strong enough to follow in his footsteps, the foreign monk thought they could be strengthened.

Back in Southern India, Bodhidharma was part of the warrior caste, a Kshatriya. Using techniques he'd learned as a warrior, he started training the Shaolin monks. Using his learned breathing techniques and movements, he unknowingly started laying the foundations for what would later be called "Kung-Fu."

This primitive form of Kung-Fu was very much stylized after Bodhidharma's Buddhist philosophies. Primarily it focused on mastering your inner self. He believed that by improving your health, focus, and the control of your mind, you could get closer to Buddha.

Bodhidharma's teachings at the Shaolin Temple led to the further development of martial art. From this infamous site, Kung-Fu spread throughout the country and eventually the world.

7 Kung-Fu Disciplines

There are hundreds of sub-disciplines under the Kung-Fu umbrella. While going through all of them in this book would not only be *near impossible*, it wouldn't help give you the foundations you need on your martial arts journey. Instead, you will see seven of the most popular and basic disciplines that will be the perfect base to start with.

1. Baguazhang

Originating in nineteenth-century China, Baguazhang, or "eight trigram palm," is a soft style of Kung-Fu. This refers to its technique which emphasizes using an opponent's power and weight against them. This involves re-directing strikes to knock opponents off-balance. A primarily defensive style, it requires a great deal of inner peace and a clear mind to effectively employ.

What makes Baguazhang unique is its integration of a wide variety of fighting techniques into one system. It is designed to allow a practitioner to engage up to eight opponents at once.

Part of what makes Baguazhang so effective is its constant movement and intricate footwork. With a practitioner constantly moving, twisting, and contorting their body, hitting them is extremely difficult. Using these techniques eliminates the need for excessive blocking and instead allows you to use deception and evasion instead.

With opponents thrown off balance, strikes can be delivered using virtually any part of the practitioner's body. Utilizing an enemy's body weight and momentum, Baguazhang also uses throws, submissions, and grabbing techniques to neutralize an attacker.

Baguazhang training starts with strengthening the mind before learning the movements. It is an inner style of Kung-Fu. It demands the ability to center yourself spiritually and mentally. Being all about flow, like a raging river around the rocks that jut out of the water, the practitioner of this discipline needs to be able to adapt.

After reaching an adequate mental level, a martial artist must first learn the circular movements central to Baguazhang. Circle walking is believed to create a sort of vortex of natural Earth energies that can be exploited to defend oneself. There is a second, straight-line method, which adds to the diversity of this well-rounded Kung-Fu discipline.

2. Northern Praying Mantis

Suppose you've ever seen Kung-Fu displayed or represented in popular media. In that case, there is no doubt you've been exposed to the Northern China-born Praying Mantis discipline. Those representations, however, are often inaccurate and do little to portray the complexities of this three-and-a-half-century-old collection of techniques. What started with a monk observing a praying mantis kill a cicada turned into one of the core variations of martial art.

Akin to Baguazhang, Northern Praying Mantis style relies on technique and movement over raw power. Using short, somewhat jerky, recoil-like movements, the Seven Star Style variation is the most dominant and generally regarded as better than the original developed at the Shaolin Temple. Because it generates strength from the waist and core, practitioners with less physical strength can help even the odds when facing stronger opponents.

Northern Praying Mantis style focuses more on a practitioner's legs than their upper body. This makes perfect sense if you think about it. Your legs are likely the strongest part of your body. This style can deliver devastating strikes with minimal effort or strain using quick-fire core power-propelled kicks. This fits perfectly with this technique's philosophy of the efficient use of energy.

3. Tai Chi

It is one of the more popular forms of Kung-Fu. It is a discipline that you probably have been more exposed to than you realize. Think about it. Have you ever seen a group of people, very often elderly, practicing what looks like slow martial arts forms in parks? They're practicing Tai Chi.

Tai Chi is all about harmony. The controlled movements and breathing techniques are designed to generate chi, also known as life energy. That promotes benefits both inward and outward.

It is exceedingly difficult to define a discipline as complex as Tai Chi. To truly understand it, you have to practice it. Using water as inspiration, similar to Baguazhang, its curved, rounded movements are meant to re-direct energy. Unlike Baguazhang, this discipline is intended to fortify and compliment a practitioner's skills and health, not for offense or self-defense.

In many ways, the harmony that Tai-Chi provides compliments a martial artist. Practicing it can improve your flexibility, expanding your array of physical capabilities. It can strengthen your muscles, bones, and tendons. Repeating and mastering the controlled movements can improve your agility and fortify your balance. There are so many potential health benefits from the discipline that medical professionals have borrowed some of its forms and principles to treat their patients.

The endless list of potential benefits of practicing Tai Chi doesn't begin and end with the *physical*. It has been shown to improve mental health as well. The balance and harmony it is based on requires a sound mind. Luckily, that's not a prerequisite to start learning the discipline as it works to improve it in practice.

There's a mystery to Tai Chi. No one really knows where its limits lie. Its wide array of physical and mental benefits makes that limitless potential all the more intriguing to martial artists and ordinary people alike.

4. Xing Yi Quan

Try to imagine a spear and how it is wielded - picture in your head the thrusting of the sharp spearhead. Take a moment and think about how that weapon is used, how it uses subtle movements to reroute enemy attacks. The spear uses the same basic ideas behind the Xing Yi Quan Kung-Fu discipline.

While some Kung-Fu disciplines are pretty, even fancy using elegant, extravagant movements, Xing Yi Quan is much more utilitarian. Its forms are built for effectiveness in battle rather than showing off and displaying the art behind it. This seemingly simple approach hides a deep complexity. That makes learning it an earnest endeavor and should be avoided by those who can't dedicate a lot of time to it.

The complexity of Xing Yi Quan starts with the fact that it requires a relatively even mix of internal, soft power techniques with more traditional martial art forms. In other words, it requires mastering the mind and soul and physical prowess. But that's not where the complexity stops.

Consisting of a large variety of connected complex forms, learning Xing Yi Quan requires a very methodical approach. Mastering it requires repeating each in a drill-like fashion, with each step building upon the one that came before. This less-than-personal approach makes it ideal for instructing large groups at once. That led to many theories that its origin was from the military – for its training regime and the technique itself.

Practitioners of Xing Yi Quan rely heavily on direct attacks and counterattacks. They use potent punches to break through the opponent's defenses. Some sub-disciplines use quick kicks like the northern Praying Mantis Style, while others focus on joint manipulation. It is a diverse style with strong utilitarian properties making it one of the more practical Kung-Fu disciplines.

5. Shaolin Style

When you think of Kung-Fu, what comes to mind? What are the first images that flash through your mind? You probably think of old-school martial arts movies or sinewy iron muscled monks in orange robes. These are all influenced by the famous spiritual mecca of the martial art, the Shaolin Temple.

Perhaps the most famous style of Kung-Fu is Shaolin Style. Not only did it originate from the same place the martial art itself originated from after the arrival of Bodhidharma, but it is also one of the most colorful and extravagant disciplines. This has led to it bleeding into almost every facet of popular culture, from movies and television to video games and music.

The practical use of Shaolin Style Kung-Fu focuses on defeating, disabling, and disarming your opponent with various strikes and blocks. Mostly shunning the use of throws and joint manipulation, this discipline emphasizes wide stances, powerful kicks, and open and close hand punches.

Where Shaolin Style differs from many other Kung- Fu disciplines is in its many sub-disciplines. Often theatrical, these branch styles often use highly agile acrobatic moves that can dazzle onlookers. Sometimes they focus on hardening parts of the body resulting in thrilling displays of strength and pain tolerance. Other sub-disciplines are based on animals or features of the natural world.

When most of us think of Shaolin Style, the aspect that stands out the most is its sheer beauty. Truly the most artistic of all the world's martial arts. This discipline is still practiced today. Initially, this variation of Kung-Fu was known for its power and how formidable its practitioners were. Today, it transitioned into more of a form of entertainment and is mainly used to build inner strength.

6. Bajiquan

Suppose you're more interested in explosiveness, sudden powerful strikes that can shatter an opponent's defense. In that case, Bajiquan might be up your alley. It gains its formidability from the idea that the human body has inherent power and protections that can be taken advantage of in self-defense.

Bajiquan is all about getting in close to your opponent, closing the distance, and using not just your fists or feet. Knees, elbows, shoulders, and even your head are natural and powerful weapons often overlooked in other Kung-Fu disciplines. In fact, they are so strong that, if used correctly, they can offset any lack of strength or physical prowess a practitioner might have. That means that it is an ideal system for beginners or those who might be at a physical disadvantage.

The power of Bajiquan doesn't just come from which extremity you use to hit your opponent. It also focuses on learning how to generate the strongest blows possible through technique. Though it has some soft power aspects, the overwhelmingly strong power needed requires an aggressive mindset. You have to continuously advance and be as efficient as possible with your movements and strikes to save energy for impactful explosive strikes.

In order to learn Bajiquan, you first need to condition and strengthen your bones to endure the arduous training required. Plus, your bones need to be able to support the powerful strikes you will deliver in your training and in practice. Though friendly to those without expansive Kung-Fu knowledge, it is one of the most demanding disciplines to learn due to what you have to endure.

Bajiquan is used today in Chinese and Taiwanese special forces. This is due to how effective a discipline it is. It can also be deadly, making it indispensable in the arsenal of those who regularly are tasked with putting their lives on the line. Even though its origins are Chinese, its principles can also be found in martial arts in countries like Israel, Brazil, Russia, and the United States.

7. Wing Chun

One day at the Shaolin Temple, a monk, Ng Mui, watched a rat and a stork fight. Though the rat was vicious, scratching, clawing, and even biting, the bird managed to hold the vermin off. By using the combination of its wings and legs, the stork prevailed, driving off the rat.

Ng Mui was one of the most formidable warriors in all of China. She took the lessons she learned from watching the stork and rat fight to develop a new Kung-Fu discipline. Once developed, she named her new art "Wing Chun."

Young by Kung-Fu standards, Wing Chun was born from Ng Mui's desire to simplify martial art. She packed all the strengths she had learned from other disciplines and tried to eliminate their inherent weaknesses. Speed, precision, and adaptability were key in making it an effective fighting technique.

Developed to work in the densely populated and often urban environments it was born in, Wing Chun can be used in more cramped spaces. It was designed to be used in tight spaces like alleyways or stairwells. It requires the use of fast strikes and superior reflexes to hold off any assailants, even armed ones.

Though inspired by a battle to the death between a bird and rat, Wing Chun's principles are based on human anatomy. A strong understanding of how the body works and how to get the most out of it has led to a style that takes less time to learn and master than other Kung-Fu disciplines. Unlike other styles, it can be adapted to different body types. There's a long history of women actually being more skilled Wing-Chun fighters.

Wing Chun, like traditional Shaolin Styles, is often heavily featured in pop culture. One of the most famous products, actually an off-shoot of the discipline, was Hollywood action movie star Bruce Lee. Using its philosophies and principles, he created a looser, more freestyle version called Jeet Kun Do. His version was more like jazz. There's more improvisation, and it has a natural flow to the way moves are made.

The most famous traditional Wing Chun fighter, and the one who saved it from almost being lost in the annals of history in the midst of the Chinese Cultural Revolution, is Ip Man. He became a rare modern Kung-Fu legend. Ip Man's fights and life have been immortalized in an extremely successful film franchise and countless books.

Chapter 2: Shaolin Kung Fu vs. Other Styles

Kung Fu is a term that can be used to encompass many different styles of martial arts. There are, however, six primary styles in the world. In this chapter, we'll look at how Shaolin Kung Fu compares to other Kung Fu styles. We will compare Shaolin with Wing Chun, Tai Chi, Northern Praying Mantis, Baguazhang, and Xing Yi Quan to see what makes it unique.

What Makes the Different Styles of Kung Fu Unique?

Many people have a hard time differentiating between Shaolin Kung Fu and other forms of Kung Fu. Each style is distinguished based on its origins, geography, characteristics, techniques, and philosophies. Apart from the above-mentioned Kung Fu styles, there are several other ancient styles. However, those are not commonly practiced.

Each unique style was developed depending on how the core art form was taught. While Shaolin Kung Fu is the oldest and most significant one, the other types like Wing Chun and Tai Chi have been prevalent for hundreds of years. While Shaolin Kung Fu is known for its wide stances, kicks, and hand strikes, Tai Chi is more of an internal martial art that focuses on mind and energy with slow physical movements. Similarly, other forms like Wing Chun and Northern Praying Mantis, while less popular outside of China, are a few of the most powerful self-defense techniques, thanks to their agile, close-range explosive movements and animal postures.

This chapter will compare Shaolin Kung Fu with other styles to see what makes them unique.

Understanding Shaolin Kung Fu

Shaolin Kung Fu is one of the oldest martial arts styles in China. It was developed at a Shaolin temple by Buddhist monks over 1500 years ago. The most popular form, which has been studied for centuries across Asia, is Wushu (Kung Fu Sport). However, few know that there are several other types of Kung Fu based on different schools and styles.

Shaolin Kung Fu emphasizes several techniques, including wide stances, kicks, and open-closed hand strikes. Shaolin Kung Fu is perhaps one of the most well-known and sophisticated among all Kung Fu styles.

Shaolin Kung Fu emphasizes animal styles, including tiger, leopard, snake, crane, and dragon.

Philosophy of Shaolin Kung Fu

In Shaolin Kung Fu, the practitioner aims to improve their physical and mental condition through rigorous training. In this style, the movements are very fluid in battle, which is why it is often called "The Dance of a Thousand Hands."

Shaolin Kung Fu emphasizes several characteristics, including power generation from stillness, sensitivity, stability, and speed. One of the most important things to remember about Shaolin Kung Fu is that it is a fighting style, an art form, and a life philosophy.

It is the only martial art form encompassing all combat styles, from grappling and ground fighting to long-range strikes, including kicks and punches.

Here are some of the main objectives behind Shaolin Kung Fu:

- To build strength and endurance
- To increase mental and spiritual awareness
- To learn how to use internal force known as chi/qi

Fighting Techniques and Methods of Shaolin Kung Fu

In Shaolin Kung Fu, the practitioner tries to make their opponent lose balance and stability by using low stances. This ancient style is considered one of China's best martial art forms because it makes full use of every part of the body for self-defense purposes.

Shaolin Kung Fu also emphasizes several attacking and blocking techniques, including long-distance kicks, open-closed hand strikes, and punching combinations.

Shaolin Kung Fu is renowned for using weapons such as staff, swords, knives, etc.

Wing Chun

Wing Chun is a type of Kung Fu developed by Buddhist nun Ng Mui and her student Yim Wing Chun. It is a martial art that focuses on close-quarter combat and involves several types of blocks, punches, kicks, and strikes used to take down an opponent quickly. The system has been taught in secret for generations until one of its students, Ng Chung-sok, published the first manual with his master's consent during the 1930s.

Wing Chun focuses on close-range combat, punches, defensive tactics like ducking and sidestepping, and agility. Wing Chun is particularly famous for its arm strikes that target pressure points on the body, which can help practitioners quickly knock their opponents out in a fight. It includes several types of blocks with crossed arms to nullify an attack before launching a counterattack.

Wing Chun is often referred to as one of the most powerful styles of Kung Fu because it emphasizes powerful strikes and blocks and focuses on speed.

Wing Chun is a practical form of self-defense used in real-life situations to defend oneself against attackers or muggers without causing any lasting injuries. However, one needs to practice the techniques regularly and under the supervision of an experienced teacher to properly master their skills.

Wing Chun is the only variation of Kung Fu to be named after women.

Wing Chun vs. Shaolin Kung Fu

Wing Chun is one of the most practical styles of Kung Fu to learn because it focuses on fighting from a short distance. It emphasizes speed and agility rather than powerful strikes that easily knock out an opponent or cause lasting injuries. Wing Chun practitioners use "soft" techniques during training sessions to avoid getting injured while practicing.

Today, Shaolin Kung Fu is practiced more for show rather than for self-defense purposes. However, it can be a very effective style of Kung Fu if practiced the right way.

Tai Chi

Tai chi is a form of Kung Fu that involves slow and gentle movements instead of quick strikes or blocks. It is more of a meditative art where the practitioner focuses on the spirit rather than technique. It is considered one of the best martial arts for health because it promotes muscle flexibility, body coordination, and improving breathing capacity.

Tai Chi is practiced chiefly in China and has been around for centuries. It was developed from older styles of Kung Fu, such as the Tiger-Crane style. It is a soft martial art that emphasizes defense rather than attack because practitioners use slow movements to evade an incoming strike before launching a counterattack against their opponent.

Tai Chi is an excellent style of Kung Fu to learn if you want to improve your health and physical well-being. Its gentle movements can help relieve stress, calm the mind, and increase muscle flexibility in elderly people.

Shaolin Kung Fu vs Tai Chi

Tai Chi is a soft form of martial art that can be used to defend oneself against an attacker without causing lasting injuries. Its movements are slow and gentle, making it perfect for people who want to learn Kung Fu but don't have the physical strength or stamina to practice other styles.

On the other hand, Shaolin Kung Fu is an aggressive martial art form with several powerful blocks and strikes. It is considered one of the best styles to learn because it can help improve physical strength, stamina, and mental capabilities in people who practice it regularly.

Northern Praying Mantis

Northern Praying Mantis Kung Fu is one of the most popular styles practiced in China. It was developed during the Song dynasty by Wang Lang, who wanted to create his own version after observing several praying mantis insects fighting each other for food and territory. Northern Praying Mantis focuses on speed, agility as well as quick counterattacks against opponents.

Northern Praying Mantis Kung Fu is a practical martial art that can be learned in just a few months. Still, it takes years to master appropriately and use effectively against opponents during training sessions or real-life situations without causing lasting injury.

Shaolin Kung Fu vs. Northern Praying Mantis Kung Fu

Northern Praying Mantis is an excellent form of Kung Fu to learn if you develop speed and agility in your movements. Its fast counterattacks make it one of the most practical styles. Still, its lack of powerful strikes means that one needs years of training before effectively using them during self-defense situations against an attacker without causing lasting injury.

Baguazhang

Baguazhang is a soft Kung Fu style developed in China by Dong Haichuan during the 19th century. It is considered one of the most effective styles because it utilizes all parts of your body, including arms, legs, and even the head, to counter an opponent's attack or block their strikes. Baguazhang practitioners don't use brute force to attack their opponents. Instead, they try to stay calm and focus on evading an incoming strike before launching a counterattack.

Baguazhang is considered one of the most graceful styles because it uses circular movements combined with quick steps to defend against an attacker's strikes without causing lasting injury during situations that require self-defense.

It is an internal form of martial art suitable for people who want to learn Kung Fu but don't have the physical strength required to practice other styles.

Baguazhang means "eight trigram palm," referring to the trigrams of the I-Ching, a Chinese classic text written thousands of years ago. The style's movements are based on the theory behind them. Its practitioners spend many years learning how to use their hands to deflect an incoming strike before launching their counterattack against opponents during training sessions or self-defense situations without causing lasting injury.

It is one of the most popular styles practiced in China today. Dong Haichuan first demonstrated Baguazhang at the Beijing opera house, where he defeated several attackers without using any weapons or physical force.

Shaolin Kung Fu vs. Baguazhang

Baguazhang is an internal form of Kung Fu that focuses on defense rather than attack. Its circular movements combined with quick steps make it one of the most graceful styles. Still, its lack of powerful strikes means that practitioners need years of training before they can effectively use them during self-defense situations without causing lasting injury or damage to their opponent.

Xing Yi Quan

Zhang Sanfeng developed it during the 14th century, and it is based on Taoist theory that says all things share common life energy, which can be controlled using breathing patterns and mental capabilities. The style focuses on quick movements combined with powerful strikes to defeat opponents without causing lasting injury during self-defense situations.

Xing Yi Quan means "Form and Intention," referring to the need to use both body movements combined with mental capabilities to understand your opponent's actions during training sessions or real-life situations.

Xing Yi Quan is an external Kung Fu style that has many practical applications during self-defense situations. Practitioners spend years perfecting their muscle movements, breathing patterns, and mental capabilities to understand the theory behind each form of attack before they attempt them against an opponent to avoid lasting injuries.

Shaolin Kung Fu vs. Xing Yi Quan

Xing Yi Quan is an external form of martial art that focuses on attacking opponents rather than defending yourself against them. Its quick movements combined with powerful strikes make it one of the most aggressive styles. Still, its lack of defensive moves means that practitioners need to spend years perfecting their muscle movements before they can effectively use them during self-defense.

Bajiquan

Bajiquan is a popular Chinese martial art that was developed during the Tang Dynasty. This style of Kung Fu focuses on explosive short-range strikes or punches with elbows or shoulders.

The term "Baji" can be translated into "eight poles" or, more literally, "eight dividing sections." This refers to the eight divisions of the body which are used during training sessions.

Bajiquan is an external style that focuses on using punches to attack opponents rather than kicks or other moves. Its quick movements combined with powerful strikes make it one of the most aggressive styles. Still, its lack of defensive moves means that practitioners need to spend years perfecting their muscle movements before they can effectively use them during self-defense.

Jin, a power delivery method, is at the very core of Bajiquan. Jin and the eight hitting methods are the essences of Bajiquan.

Shaolin Kung Fu vs Bajiquan

Bajiquan is an external style that focuses on attacking opponents rather than defending yourself against them. Its quick movements combined with powerful strikes make it one of the most aggressive styles.

Benefits of Kung Fu Practice

Kung Fu has many benefits such as:

- Building strength and stamina

- Improving flexibility

- Increasing bone density to prevent fractures in old age. Kung Fu training can reduce the risk of falls among older people by up to 20 percent. This is because it trains your mind and body coordination, balance, and equilibrium which helps you maintain good posture and ultimately avoid falls.

- Teaching self-control, discipline, patience, and respect for others. Kung Fu training can help improve your awareness of the world around you and give you a sense of purpose in life. It also encourages people to interact with each other during sessions, creating a sense of belonging within different communities worldwide.

Which Kung Fu Style Should You Learn

There are many different styles of Kung Fu, including Shaolin, Wing Chun, Tai Chi, Northern Praying Mantis, and Baguazhang. The best martial art style you should learn depends on your reason for wanting to do it in the first place. Some people want to do it purely for looks. They love how Kung Fu moves look when practiced, whereas others want to do it because they enjoy the challenge of learning a new sport.

You should also consider how much time and effort you are willing to put into training. For instance, some styles of Kung Fu require less physical strength than others but still provide plenty of benefits for your mind and body if practiced correctly.

What is the Deadliest Kung Fu Style?

Wing Chun may be the deadliest style of Kung Fu because it is an external form that focuses on defensive moves designed to counter opponents' attacks. Wing Chun uses many kicking techniques and hand movements and blocks, making it one of the most effective styles when fighting against opponents who use different physical combat methods.

Most Practical Kung Fu Style for Self Defense

Wing Chun is the most practical style of Kung Fu for self-defense because it focuses on using defensive moves designed to counter attacks. Wing Chun uses many kicking techniques and hand movements and blocks, making it one of the most effective styles when fighting against opponents who use different physical combat methods.

Deciding which Kung Fu style to learn depends on your reason for wanting to do it in the first place and how much time and effort you are willing to put into training. The availability of master trainers can also play a big part in what style of Kung Fu you decide to learn.

Kung Fu and the Modern World

Kung Fu is a traditional Chinese martial art style that dates back hundreds of years. Its history can be traced way back to 500 BC when Bodhidharma, also known as Ta Mo in China, created what some people believe to be the first Kung Fu school.

The sport has evolved into an extremely popular practice around the world with an estimated 200 million practitioners. It has made its way into modern-day martial arts, appearing in films such as Kill Bill and Enter the Dragon.

Kung Fu became more popular when it was introduced into the modern martial arts world. It has since been incorporated into other styles of fighting that have become very well known throughout media around the world, including Krav Maga, which is a mix between Kung fu, and Karate moves.

This style started to get used in movies during the 1970s and has since been used in countless films and TV shows such as Crouching Tiger, Hidden Dragon (2000), The Matrix trilogy (1999-2003), and the Ip Man series.

Some modern martial arts, such as Taekwondo and Karate, were developed from traditional styles of Kung Fu. However, some people believe that some forms of Kung Fu are not practical for self-defense because some moves cannot be used in a real situation.

The Popularity of Kung Fu Styles in Western Countries

Kung Fu has become very popular among western countries over the last few years due to its incorporation into many different modern martial arts forms used in movies and TV shows. These days, you can even take Kung Fu classes in some gyms.

However, people might not realize that there are hundreds, if not thousands, of Kung Fu styles, and not all of them are suitable for self-defense. Some styles focus on using defensive moves that counterattacks, whereas others focus on attacking the enemy or protecting themselves from harm.

Some styles of Kung Fu are more popular in Western countries compared to other forms, which can be linked to the availability of master trainers, available training time, and how well-known the style is across media.

Shaolin Kung Fu and Tai Chi are two of the most popular styles in Western countries, whereas Wing Chun and Northern Praying Mantis are less well-known.

Kung Fu styles evolved, and numerous styles came to be practiced for their varying benefits. Today, seven styles are still practiced. Some focus more on attacking the enemy or protecting from harm, whereas others focus on using defensive moves to counter attacks.

All the Kung Fu styles focus on posture and footwork, internal and external training of the body. These styles aim to provide health benefits like improved muscle tone and increased flexibility, among many others.

Kung Fu has evolved from a martial art into an exercise regime for good health, which is why so many people in Western countries are taking classes to improve their fitness.

Shaolin Kung Fu and Tai Chi are two of the most popular styles in Western countries, whereas Wing Chun and Northern Praying Mantis are less well-known. Deciding which style to learn depends on why you want to get into Kung Fu, as well as how much time you're willing to put into training.

Chapter 3: The 5 Animal Patterns of Kung Fu

Inspiration for the different Kung Fu disciplines often came from a multitude of sources. Some were developed out of a simple need for self-defense. The China that many of these disciplines originated in was a violent place. Feudal Lords were often at war, leaving the citizens to bear the brunt of the effects and deal with roving gangs of bandits or wayward soldiers determined to take, rape, maim, and sometimes even kill.

One of the main drivers of developing Kung Fu styles was self-improvement. Spurred on by the teachings of The Yellow King, segments of the Chinese population were motivated to become better. This included a focus on mental health as well as physical health. Aligning the two became crucial for people to find the balance necessary to become the best versions of themselves.

As shown by Bodhidharma, religious piety can be bolstered by practicing martial arts. One of the most popular paths to understanding Buddha's Nature came in the form of Kung Fu. The meditative and humble nature of its many disciplines is inspired by providing a wide selection of possible choices that fit a practitioner's needs and attributes.

Lastly, one of the most well-known inspirations for the different Kung Fu styles comes from nature itself. That wasn't limited by elemental forces like the wind, fire, water, and earth. Animals were observed, copied, and learned from to develop five main animal-inspired techniques that eventually became synonymous with martial arts.

Let's take a look at the five animal patterns and techniques significant to Kung Fu.

Tiger

Tiger

The largest cat and one of the most formidable predators in all of nature is the Tiger. Today, the tiger population is slowly declining, and it is being added to the list of endangered species. However, in

Ancient China, they were far from endangered. These dangerous creatures were a real threat to farmers and travelers alike. With that danger came profound respect. Kung Fu practitioners steadily developed an admiration for the fearlessness of tigers. Their courage and fierceness represent inner strength, which helps lead one towards straightforward forms with clear intent. This makes one courageous and a force to be reckoned with.

Style and Technique

Kung Fu practitioners find inspiration in one of the most vicious weapons at a tiger's disposal, which is their claws. The tiger style utilizes very strong hand movements and techniques, the "tiger fist." A practitioner's hands are actually formed into a claw-like shape to mimic the big cat. In order to turn their hands into something just as tough as the talons at the ends of the massive creature's paws, a tough, painful training process had to be employed.

Several popular training techniques are used to strengthen one's hand when practicing the Tiger style. One such technique is often referred to as the "Clawing Jar." With your hand folded in a tiger fist, grab a large empty glass or a ceramic jar. Fill the vessel with water up to its brim. You can also fill it to just half to practice in the beginning. Try to move it around in your hand as much as you can for about five to ten minutes. Every day, add another cup and keep adding until the jar is filled to the top. Next, repeat the same process with sand. This training will help strengthen and fortify every part of your hand and parts of your arms. It is simple, and you can easily find everything you need at home to practice and build your skill.

Exercises

Another exercise to build up a powerful tiger fist is called "Taming the Tiger," in which you build up the muscles and tendons in your fingers. Start by getting into a push-up position. Extend out your fingers until they're supporting your entire body's weight. With your fingers still extended, bend your arms, and lower your body to bring it close to the floor (but do not let it touch the surface). After holding your body in this position for a few seconds, pull it back up to return to your original position.

You can practice Taming the Tiger at your own pace and perform as many reps at once as you want. However, increase the number of counts and time period every time you practice. Take at least one hour every day to practice and try to do at least thirty to fifty of these finger-supported push-ups before getting to the actual training. One popular Tiger-style training technique is called the "Piercing Beans." The first thing you need to do is get your tiger fists (hands) in a tub or a basket as wide as your shoulders and filled with dry beans.

Get into the horse stance position and keep your spine straight. Both thighs need to be parallel to the ground, the mat, or the floor. Lift your hands, stick your fingers out straight (keep them rigid), and thrust them alternatively into the container of beans. Try to hold back the power you're putting into this motion. Besides being designed to strengthen your hands, this exercise will also help you naturally generate more strength and build muscle memory. Repeat it a few times.

Dragon

Dragon

The dragon represents the mystical and spiritual energy in Kung Fu. The three empowering or fundamental entities of this martial art are jing (internal force), chi (intrinsic energy), and shen (mind power), which collectively make one unit and thrive in harmony. They are known as the "three treasures." Despite being a mythical creature, the dragon is taken seriously in Chinese culture and philosophy. The animal represents one's fighting spirit and converts its energy into a physical force. It also stresses the importance of flexibility and grace, thereby representing the "chi" energy.

Characteristics and Symbolization

The dragon represents prosperity, success, and luck. Hailing from water, the creature holds an important position in Chinese mythology. Its flowing movements and undulating force are well-respected in Shaolin Kung Fu. In fact, some of the toughest moves in this martial art are inspired by the swift movement of the Dragon. Its water-borne identity helps one develop inner strength and bring flexibility in their moves. Shen refers to "spirit" or "mind," and the Dragon motivates practitioners to build internal strength. At the same time, it also inspires them to stay mentally healthy, fresh, and peaceful to practice Kung Fu with grace.

The Dragon is extremely powerful and works at its own will. It can appear or disappear at any time and transcend into a supernatural state whenever it pleases. Dragons are strong, unpredictable, and deceptive. The four Shaolin animals collectively represent internal and external strength and combine several kicks and fists combinations. It is necessary to stay relaxed and focused on your movements when taking inspiration from the dragon to improve your skill. By contrast, the dragon can be extremely dangerous or act as a pacifist when unhappy or surrounded by negative energy. This opposing characteristic is also reflected in their exercises and technique.

Exercises and Techniques

The two famous moves in Kung Fu inspired by the dragon are "Dragon Claw" and "Dragon-tail Kick." Both training drills use quick movements, snapping kicks, and full fists as their main strategy. The techniques also combine several movements and exercises from other animals. Basically, masters train practitioners to become more agile, flexible, and strong. "Swimming Dragon Plays with Water" and "Green Dragon Shoots Pearls" are two other techniques related to the dragon. As mentioned, the moves inspired by the dragon can be confusing. You are moving gently with grace at one instance, and at the other, you are completely in action and ready to strike the opponent.

Basically, you can adapt to every move, technique, and fight based on your surroundings and the opponent you are fighting with. You are the complete opposite of the other person, which gives you enough flexibility and freedom to win the fight. Typical dragon-style Kung Fu warriors react to their opponent's moves after scrutinizing their moves and counterattacking by deciphering their weak points. They are also known as counterpunchers. Northern Dragon Style and Southern Dragon Style are two types of Dragon-inspired Kung Fu.

The former skill motivates the fighter to keep their ground, while the latter keeps the fighting fluid and flexible. Some spinning evasion moves are paired with rapid kicks and blocks in Northern Dragon Style Kung Fu. On the other hand, fighters confuse and evade their opponents in Southern Style Kung Fu to win the game. The "Dragon Claw" technique is one of the most common yet unique moves in Kung Fu. It strengthens your claw power and helps you win against your opponent using the power of your hand.

To practice this move, curl your middle finger, index finger, and thumb like a pincer to grab the ligaments or tendons of your opponent to win the fight. If you are trained for it, you can also use an open palm or your palm's heel to bring your opponent down.

Crane

Crane

The crane represents poise, grace, and steadiness in Kung Fu. The techniques inspired by this animal relatively need less strength and are based on evasive movements. When calm, the bird stands elegantly on one leg. However, when it sees rising tides and winds, it takes action and pecks with precision to combat the situation. The bird inspires several Kung Fu techniques for this reason. The crane can also inspire you in your daily life. It teaches elegance and grace.

If you are clumsy or seeking to develop elegance, learn from the crane and boost your self-improvement process.

Characteristics

The crane represents the "jing" energy. It portrays essence and elegance as its main features. Ideally, the crane stays silent, poised, and calm at all times. However, when needed, it can strike with action. Even when in action, the movements are kept bare minimum and extremely straightforward. The famous Shaolin quote, "The spirit of the crane, resides within the stillness," is the main motivation behind the Kung Fu moves. The bird takes less offense and focuses on the weak points of the opponent. Despite being less popular than other animals in Kung Fu, the crane's energy and defense mechanisms are probably the strongest and basically unbeatable.

Some vital and soft areas targeted by the bird include the throat, eyes, ribs, sides of the head, and heart. Just like the crane, the practitioner needs to be tall and possess strong concentration levels. They should also have a good balance and have the ability to use as little energy as possible. More importantly, they should be able to remain still and calm for a longer period, which means that they should be extremely patient. When in crisis, the crane uses its weightlessness to keep things in control and drive results with accuracy.

Exercises and Techniques

As mentioned, practitioners need minimal strength when practicing Kung Fu techniques related to the crane. They focus on the upper body parts of the opponents during a strike. Critical areas like the throat and the eyes are the primary attack points. The techniques are also based on self-defense mechanisms that give the practitioners optimum strength and help them keep their opponents off balance. A famous soft style exercise inspired by this animal is the "Crane Beak." Practitioners finding trouble in gaining strength or the ones who are physically weak can rely on the Crane Beak technique to win their game.

When practicing this technique, you need to bunch your index finger, middle finger, and thumb together to make a hook-like shape resembling a crane's beak. You then need to focus on just one point and sway your hand into a pecking motion with a thrusting force. Kicks are also an integral part of the crane-related Kung Fu movements. Combined with the "Phoenix-Eye Fist," Crane Beak moves become stronger as they collectively attack the vital points. "Satisfied Reincarnated Crane" and "Crane Stands Amongst Cockerels" are two other forms or techniques developed from the crane's pose and movements.

Snake

Snake

As the Shaolin saying goes, "Hard like steel and soft like a rope of silk," the snake can be strong and deceptive. It is fast, agile, precise, and accurate in its moves. It can easily intimidate people by hissing at them but not necessarily attacking them. The reptile stays aware at all times and can scare its enemies by repeating coiling motions and utilizing its thin yet quick muscles. It can also easily hide from them, thereby giving it a chance to attack with precision. Every move and bite from the snake is poisonous, which is why the one on the receiving end must be more aware when tackling the creature.

Symbolization

The snake represents "chi" energy, which relates to profound sensitivity and awakening. The creature is aware at all times and therefore ready to attack its opponents at any given point in time. It is known as the "earth dragon" and glides smoothly to achieve its goals. The spirit and energy are intricately connected, just like the serpent's characteristics. It thrives in harmony with the chi energy, which collectively represents endurance and fluidity. It drives one's internal force and keeps the practitioners' movements smooth. When the snake is completely aware, it can use all of its muscle power and memory to make targeted strikes.

The serpent also acts as a revelation to promote good values in your everyday life. For example, it instills the importance of being grounded, precise in your moves, and more self-aware. It also symbolizes luck and health. It inspires you to keep training and working hard. Your weaknesses can be turned into your strength if you are dedicated and consistent. In Chinese astrology, the serpent is an important symbol used by the emperor. The snake also portrays certain signs possessed by the other four animals in Shaolin Kung Fu, thereby creating harmony among all creatures.

Techniques

One of the most popular techniques inspired by the serpent is the "Snake Hand form," which is a powerful defense technique. It uses one or two fingers to exert a thrusting force on the opponents. This movement can also take every opponent by surprise as it is extremely agile and explosive. The practitioner must work on building their muscles as the technique demands major muscle power. They should also be quick on their feet and build a thin silhouette for swift movements. The main body parts attacked through this technique include the throat, face, and eyes, considered the opponents' weak points.

The "Snake Hand" and "Spear Hand" are two other popular techniques in Kung Fu inspired by the serpent. Some other lesser-known techniques are "Snake Basking in Mist," "White Snake Crosses Valley," and "Poisonous Snake Shoots Venom." An important part of training for the serpent techniques in Kung Fu includes the development of self-awareness. Some trainers ask their students to build self-awareness and improve focus. This can help them become more aware of their subconscious thoughts and surroundings, which is necessary to improve self-defense and beat opponents with precision. This, in turn, also saves a lot of energy.

Leopard

Leopard

The leopard in Shaolin Kung Fu represents the saying, "Bend fingers hard, like iron." The leopard represents speed, calculation, efficiency, stealth, and strength. Leopards are also known for their hunting skills and high speed, especially when covering a short distance. When they spot prey, leopards hide or lurk stealthily, ready to pounce. Without alerting their prey, they look for the perfect moment to attack the smaller animal.

Characteristics

The leopard symbolizes instantaneous speed. Its moves are explosive in nature, and it focuses on counterattacks to win the game. It signifies the "Li" energy, which stresses the importance of muscular strength. When you train as a leopard, you can easily combat everyday struggles and move swiftly through your daily tasks. You can also notice an increase in your speed as you tackle important tasks and take necessary actions. Some compare the characteristics and techniques of the leopard with the tiger as both belong to the same family. However, there is a major difference between both animals in terms of movements and efficiency.

The tiger focuses on power and strength, whereas the leopard pays attention to precision and quickness. Just like a leopard, practitioners need to build supple strength to pounce easily and retract their limbs to throw an efficient strike. The leopard is brave, courageous, and fierce. Instead of being scared, the animal intimidates its opponents by simply showing up. The practitioner also needs to build torso strength and develop agility around their waist as that area helps them make swift movements. At the same time, high speed and power are the two other qualities the practitioner must improve on and maintain.

Techniques

The main strategy deployed by Kung Fu moves related to the leopard is *stealth and quickness.* Just like the leopard attacks with speed, Kung Fu practitioners attack to inflict pain to distract their opponents and thrust a major blow to go for the kill. In a way, they use distraction to win. The main attacking areas are the armpits, groin, neck, ears, and temples, which are basically all the regions with soft tissues. The practitioner must build strength and develop muscles to pounce on their opponent to inflict pain and cause distraction. Another requirement is supple strength. "Golden

Leopard Watches Fire" and "Golden Leopard Speeds through Forest" are some of the other typical techniques.

The main technique used in this form of Kung Fu is the "Leopard Paw," in which the practitioner makes a half fist and attacks the opponent with two knuckles. This blow is intense and can make painful contact with the surface. Sharpening the Leopard Paw technique is extremely crucial as it is the first instinct of any attack. The stronger the blow is, the weaker the opponent becomes to fight right from the beginning. It should be lightning-fast, efficient, and sharp. Masters suggest that their students work hard on improving their precision as the strike should be placed at accurate spots and points.

Chapter 4: Stances in Kung Fu

There are several stances in Kung Fu, and most of them are derived from the five primary stances. This chapter focuses on five stances: the Horse Stance, Cat Stance, Forward Stance, Twist Stance, and Crane Stance. It begins by outlining the importance of stances in Kung Fu and also highlights other positions that may be of interest to you.

Significance of Stances in Kung Fu

Stances play a fundamental role when you are practicing Shaolin Kung Fu. They form the basis of learning this type of martial art, but most students usually take a long time to realize their importance. On the first day of learning Shaolin Kung Fu, every student is introduced to basic stances, including Forward Stance, Horse Stance, and Cat stance. During the introductory lesson, most students will develop a keen interest in knowing more about these stances. At this stage, the student becomes eager to learn high kicks, some fancy movements, and other fighting techniques.

After training for a long time, this is when you can fully appreciate the significance of stances in Shaolin Kung Fu. While the stances are basic and are usually taught in the first lesson, constant training determines whether you have mastered the skill of properly applying them or not. Novices are usually interested in watching the hand movements, but experienced practitioners observe the stances and bodywork when they view performance. The stances drive the hand motions, which give them power.

Furthermore, the stances are crucial because they allow you to use your body effectively. With a proper stance, you can control the motion of your body. All body movements pass through various stances, which help provide hand techniques and a solid foundation for coordinating different parts of the body. The stances also help you harness ground power when you execute various moves. The following section discusses the basic stances of Shaolin Kung Fu.

Horse Stance

The Horse Stance is the first stance you will learn when you start your journey in learning Kung Fu. The Horse Stance basically means horse-riding stance, and it represents a wide squat. You can easily get into this stance where you stand with your feet and make sure they are positioned wide apart. The width of your shoulder should be parallel to your feet. When you are in this stance, bend your knees and try to rest your body down.

Horse Stance

This stance constitutes basic training for different styles used in Kung Fu. First and foremost, the Horse stance plays a crucial role in strengthening the legs. To be an effective fighter, your legs should have sufficient power to maintain your balance. In other words, the major purpose of this stance is endurance training, which helps strengthen the tendons and leg muscles. It also teaches students how to relax in their stance in such a way that their center of gravity is low. There is no need to push the chest outward in this position. This is essential since the power in Kung Fu is obtained from the ground. Students can also sit in a particular stance when practicing different hand moves. For instance, you can use it to practice punches while at the same time learning how to evade attacks.

When you practice this stance, make sure you keep your feet out, and they should be wider than your shoulders. While maintaining your feet facing forward, slowly squat into a position that resembles a person riding a horse. Make sure that your posture is flat and the spine is in a straight position. How low you get in this stance significantly varies depending on the Kung Fu style you want to practice.

If you want to train using the Horse stance, you should first get a stick and assume the position. While in this position, put the stick on top of your knees and hold your arms outward. The palms should be parallel to your body. You should not allow the stick to fall. Repeat the exercise until you familiarize yourself with this stance.

Forward Stance

This is a crucial step in Shaolin Kung Fu. It is useful for moving your body forward, and it helps form a stable base to allow you to generate power and perform advanced movements. When you are attacking an opponent, you must utilize this stance to ensure that you are in a proper position. Your weight will be on the front leg, and it determines the action you will take.

Forward Stance

In this stance, bend your front knee while your back leg is straight. When you view the stance from the side, it will look like a drawn bow. As such, its other name is the bow stance. Others prefer to call it the forward-leaning stance, and it is used in different styles of martial arts. The shoulders and hips should remain facing forward. Essentially, the main purpose of this stance is to teach the practitioner musculoskeletal alignment, which plays a crucial role in adding the earth's mass to the strike. With this stance, you have a great chance of generating forward power. However, very little power can be generated in the reverse direction.

In Kung Fu, the Front Stance is practiced using different variations depending on the particular style you wish to undertake. The other function of the stance is to give you stability while you project the weight of your body forward. This often happens when punching to deliver a powerful blow to your opponent. When you strike, you should make sure that the punch is strong enough to have a competitive advantage over the opponent.

Your straight rear leg will push the center of gravity forward to ensure that the body's full weight is behind your strike. In this case, the bent front leg will help support body weight. Additionally, you can also use the front stance to move forward or backward as long as you are sure that the center of gravity or bodyweight is projected forward. The center of gravity is critical since it determines the power of the strike and its impact on the victim. In contrast, the back stance is used when you place the weight of your body on the rear leg. For instance, you assume this position when you lean backward to evade an attack.

Cat Stance

Cat Stance

The Cat Stance is primarily meant for mobility and other transitional movements from one position to the other. All your body weight will be on your back leg while the front leg will rest on the ball of the foot of the toe. Your front leg should resemble the way a cat puts its paw out when it takes a step. There will be no weight on the paw, and this is where the name came from. You can use the front leg to shift to another stance or to kick your opponent.

It is still fine if you start your stance from a higher level then move down slowly with your training. This stance is versatile, and it allows you to move quickly and to remain light on your feet. When using this stance, you must visualize the cat as it readies to swiftly spring forward swiftly to catch its prey. You should aim to do the same when you use this particular style.

If you want to practice the left cat stance, step the right foot back from the starting position. Turn the right foot you moved back clockwise at an angle of about 45 degrees so that you can get a better balance. The next move is to bend your right knee in such a way that you place about 90% of your weight on that leg. Your left foot should reach out in front, and you use the ball of the foot to place it on the ground. Do not use the base of the foot when grounding your left foot. You will only place very little downward pressure using your left leg. The benefit of this move is that little harm will be caused if the opponent tries the trick of sweeping your lead leg. Furthermore, you can also use your lead leg to avoid the sweep.

The Cat Stance offers excellent balance when you use it as a front kick snap in such a way that you keep the opponent at bay. Since there is little weight exerted on your front leg, you can quickly deploy it and use the ball of your foot as a weapon. The stance is an effective way of attacking your opponent if you use it as self-defense.

Twist Stance

The Twist Stance is a transitional stance, and your legs will appear twisted to help you execute your next move. Your front foot should be turned outward, while your back foot should be resting on the front foot's ball. You can use this stance to advance toward the opponent or to retreat when you realize that you are under pressure. You can also use it to change the position of the body. If you want to change direction, you untwist the legs and resume the stance once positioned correctly.

Twist Stance

You can also use the twist stance to execute a concealed sidekick. It is good in that it helps you get good balance which helps you perform various moves when facing the opponent. When the opponent attempts to sweep your front leg, you can keep your balance because of the little weight on that side. Furthermore, you can counter the attack by attempting another sweep on the opponent. The stance is also used to dodge low attacks.

The Twist Stance is useful in several ways, depending on how you want to use it. The way you get into this stance or come out of it determines how you can effectively use it. You can pivot into many throws or utilize your twisting momentum to bring the opponent down. You can also perform a sweeping technique when your hands move in the opposite direction.

Crane Stance

The Crane Stance resembles the way a crane stands on one leg. With this stance, you stand on one leg while the other one is raised. The stance is commonly used in Kung Fu and other forms of martial arts since it helps develop body coordination and balance. Essentially, the stance is focused on training the student to maintain balance while standing on one leg.

Crane Stance

You can use the stance to kick the opponent or evade and attack. When you kick the opponent using this stance, you can reach higher. You can also use it to perform sidekicks while maintaining the balance of your body on one leg. You build this stance by raising your knee to its maximum height while facing the opponent.

Remember that, with the crane stance, your supporting leg should be bent at knee level. This helps you maintain balance and enhance the execution of your kicks. If you lock your knee, it becomes very easy to lose balance, creating room for the opponent to attack. You may also have trouble performing follow-up techniques if your knee is locked. Eventually, this will render your stance useless.

The sidekick that you execute from a Crane Stance can be combined with a back strike. When you use your sidekick on the opponent, they will fall toward you, and this is when you can strike their head with a back fist. If you follow this stance and execute your kicks well, you will gain a competitive advantage over your opponent.

These are the five basic stances in Shaolin Kung Fu you should know if you want to become a master in this martial art. As you progress through your training, you will realize that there are also several other stances you must know. The following are some of the stances that you may need to know as you advance in your journey of mastering Kung Fu.

Bow Stance

Bow Stance

The bow stance is a variation of the forward stance, and it plays a critical role in Kung Fu. This basic stance involves moving your body forward, which gives you the stability to generate more power and advance your movement. When you are in this stance, you can pivot the center of your weight on the front leg to ensure maximum force when you hit your target. Your back leg should be straight, while your front knee should be bent. If you view this stance from the side, it looks like a drawn bow, which is why it is also known as the bow stance. You should make sure that both heels line up. Do not forget the back heel when you move forward.

Lower Stance

Most Kung Fu students don't like this stance because it requires you to assume a very wide horse stance. You will place the entire weight of your body on one leg, and you should squat as low as you can.

This stance is primarily meant to help you avoid high attacks, knee, ankle, and groin attacks. Since you will be squatting very low in this stance, it tends to exert some pressure on your lower muscles which can cause pain.

If you are looking forward to learning Kung Fu, your first lesson will cover different stances. You must pay attention to these stances since they affect almost every move you make, and coordinate elements like body movement and footwork. Therefore, you should not neglect different stances as they affect almost everything you do in Kung Fu.

Chapter 5: The Lohan Pattern

The Lohan Pattern is one of the most important aspects of Kung Fu. It is a series of 18 hand movements used for many purposes, including self-defense and their health benefits. The Lohan pattern comes from Buddhist scripture but has been modified over the years to fit different styles of Kung Fu. In this article, we will discuss each movement in detail to become more familiar with them.

Origin of the Lohan Pattern

The Lohan Pattern was first introduced to the Shaolin monks in the 18th century when Daai Yuk came across Buddhist scripture that detailed hand movements described as "18 Hands of Luohan". This became known as The Lohan pattern and has been used in many styles of Kung Fu ever since then.

According to an ancient legend, a Buddhist monk, Bodhidharma, credited as the founder of Shaolin Kung Fu, meditated for many years to reach enlightenment. During this time, he had lost all his energy and strength because of his lack of movement. He decided that if he were to regain these powers, it would be through rigorous exercises. These exercises were designed to teach others how they too can improve their health and spiritual well-being.

The Lohan Pattern is meant to be one of the foundations in Wushu training because it helps develop a person's awareness and coordination through movement. It also teaches how to defend oneself when necessary, which can become useful for many different reasons (i.e., self-defense or if you're attacked). The patterns are meant to be forms of meditation where your mind can focus on the movements. You can relieve stress, improve coordination, and have a more focused mindset by practicing these hand patterns.

Importance of Lohan Hand Patterns for Kung Fu

Understanding Lohan hand patterns can help you improve your Kung Fu. It is a series of 18 exercises originally meant to develop strength, flexibility, and coordination within the body. However, many schools have modified them over time to work on self-defense skills as well. For example, some movements are used to trap or grapple opponents, while others help relax the body after fighting.

The number 18 is significant in Buddhism, so The Lohan Pattern has become an integral part of Kung Fu. Though everyone may have their own interpretation of it, each style emphasizes knowing these patterns inside and out. By gaining a complete understanding of this pattern, you will improve your Kung Fu skills.

These hand patterns are also called Qigong exercises and were kept secret for many years in the famous Shaolin Temple. Though they were shared with monks and other Kung Fu masters, the movements were kept secret so no one could copy their fighting style.

The Importance of Chi Kung for Kung Fu

Chi kung (also known as Qi gong) is an aspect of Kung Fu that focuses on cultivating and controlling energy throughout the body. This includes harnessing it to make your body stronger, more flexible, or even heal certain ailments.

Chi has been around for many years but was first mentioned in ancient China by the Yellow Emperor. He stated that there were two energies within all living things: Yin and Yang. Yin is considered to be female energy, while Yang is male energy. They work together in harmony to create Chi (energy). This can then lead to good health and even enlightenment if harnessed correctly.

The Lohan Pattern is one of many exercises that can help you with your Chi Kung. Performing these movements helps improve flexibility, strength, and coordination, eventually leading to better Kung Fu skills.

For Wushu enthusiasts, this means that they must learn how to perform these hand patterns to become better martial artists.

Practicing the Lohan Pattern

The Lohan Pattern is often mistaken for merely physical exercise. However, it is much more than that. It is a Chi Kung exercise, which engages both the mind and the body to achieve miraculous results.

It is therefore vital to learn how to perform this pattern correctly. The most common mistake is the lack of focus and concentration when performing these movements. You must put your heart into it to better understand the purpose of learning Kung Fu in general.

To gain maximum benefits out of the Lohan exercises, they should be performed along with Chi Kung breathing. This will help build the energy within your body and allow you to feel a stronger connection with each movement.

Importance of Practicing with a Master

The exercises described in this chapter are merely physical forms of the exercise. To get the full benefit of practice, learning more about the mind and energy is crucial. The masters of Shaolin teach these techniques of the internal dimension. Hence, whenever possible, you should practice with a master of Shaolin Kung Fu.

The Basics of the Lohan Patterns

Here is a brief explanation of the 18 movements with some images to help you better understand them.

Lifting the Sky

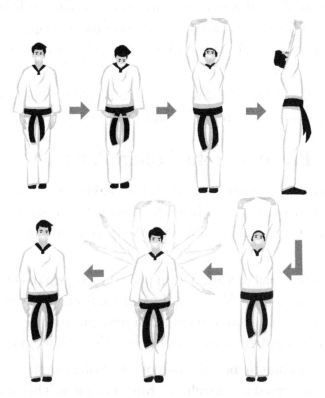

The first pattern begins with both hands reaching up to the sky. They are then brought down on either side of your body.

This means that you must stretch out forward and raise your arms above your head as if picking something heavy like a sack of rice. When doing this exercise, your palms should be facing upward, which is the opposite of what you might expect.

After reaching up, the hands are brought down on either side of your torso to form a level line with both arms fully extended.

Shooting Arrows

Shooting Arrows

The next movement is where things get a little more complicated. Here, one hand shoots out while the other pulls back in an arrow-like fashion.

A common mistake here is to move both hands together so they are parallel or even pointing slightly downwards. Instead, make sure to move one arm at a time. This ensures that you are properly engaging your core muscles while performing this exercise.

Plucking Stars

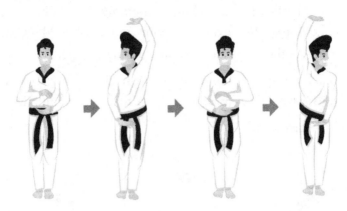

Extend one hand skyward, palm facing up, and extend the other hand downward, palm facing down. Keep your arms close to your body and stretch out skyward.

You should then bring that arm back to your side while extending the opposite arm in an upward motion.

As your hand reaches the top of its movement, it should be palm facing up while your other arm is still at your side. When you bring that arm back to rest, extend the other one in a downward motion again.

Turning Head

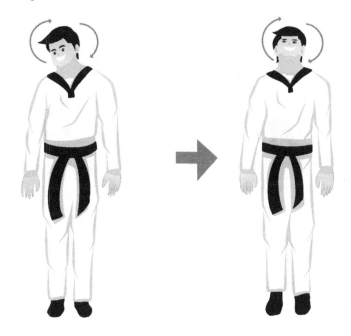

Turning Head

Rotate your head in a circular fashion as if you are turning your head around to look at the sky.

The head is a very important part of this exercise as it connects our mind with our body. Therefore, make sure that you keep your neck straight and do not awkwardly push or pull forward when performing these movements.

This pattern is known to have numerous benefits for the nervous system.

Merry-Go-Round

Merry-Go Round

Bring your hands together, join them and intertwine your fingers. Now imagine you are holding a stick in your hand. Circulate your arms, outstretched, around your body. Move from your waist.

This exercise works well to wake you up and stimulate your blood flow.

Thrust Punch

Thrust Punch

Assume a wide stance, toes pointing in 180-degree angles. Now, just like practicing a punch, thrust your arms forward with one arm on top of the other.

As you move them out, extend both fists together to form an L shape in front of your body. Then bring it back down to rest by crossing both hands over each other at chest level while still keeping a wide stance.

The Thrust Punch pattern is a great exercise for your heart, lungs, kidneys, and digestive system.

Carrying the Moon

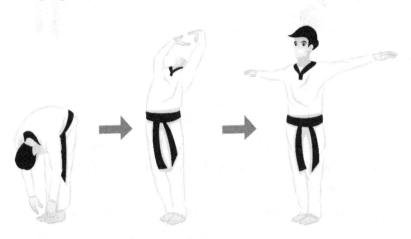

Carrying the Moon

This pattern starts with you bending forward at the waist without bending your knees. Try to bend as far as possible towards your toes. Now, in the next step, lift your arms skyward to perform the core position. In the final step, separate your hands by bringing them down sideways.

This exercise boosts youth and vitality and is excellent for your back ailments.

Nourishing Kidneys

Nourishing Kidneys

Start with your arms on your waist. Bend backward. In the second step, bend at the waist and touch your toes with your fingers without bending your knees.

Kidney function is closely related to reproductive wellness. This position is crucial for fertility, vitality, and sciatica-related issues.

Three Levels to Ground

This is a basic squat where your arms are stretched out sideways. This exercise is well-known as the "frog position" and is very effective for your legs.

Doing multiple repetitions will raise your heart rate and improve cardiovascular fitness.

Dancing Crane

Bend your knees and shift your weight to one leg. Now move the other foot forward while keeping the knee bent to a 90-degree angle, forming an L shape with both legs.

This exercise is great for increasing joint flexibility and building strong bones by stimulating calcium production in the body.

Carrying Mountains

Stand in an upright position. Raise your arms sideways to a shoulder level. Now twist through your waist so that your lower body is facing the front, and your upper body (waist up) is facing sideways. Repeat this on both sides. This position is ideal for chronic back pain.

Drawing Knife

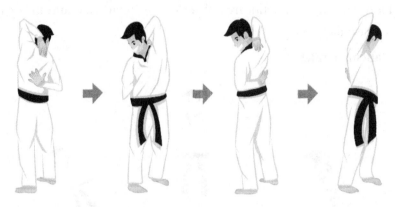

Start by standing in an upright position, feet together. Hold stance. Now imagine holding something behind your back with one arm. Raise the other arm and now put it behind your head to touch the other arm. Imagine pulling out an arrow from your quiver.

Presenting Claws

Presenting Claws

In a wide stance, raise your hands to your chest, palms facing outward. Now bend your fingers like claws. This is your starting position. In the second step, move one hand to your side and raise the other skyward. Now to reach the final position, bend sideways at the waist so that the raised hand bends in the opposite direction over your head. Repeat for the other side.

Pushing Mountains

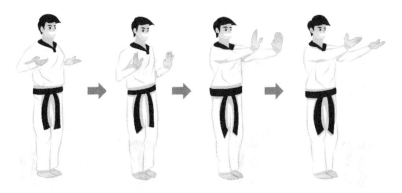

Pushing Mountains

Keep your knees slightly bent. As if you were pushing against a wall, push the palms of both hands together, like they were stuck to each other.

This pattern is great for relieving mental stress and builds strength throughout the body. It will also tone your legs and arms over time because it assists with circulation.

Separating Water

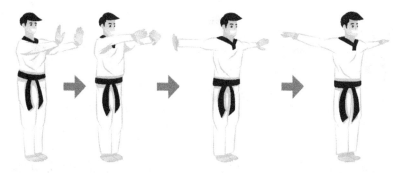

Start with your feet together, arms by the side. Now lift both arms sideways to your shoulders. Next, bring them to the front and sweep them sideways as if swimming. This pattern is very useful for developing arm strength.

Big Windmill

This is an easy one. Simply rotate your arms in 360 degrees while standing upright. Repeat for both arms.

Deep Knee Bending

A deep knee bend is nothing but a squat on your toes and arms stretched out in front of you. Arms should be parallel to the ground. This is also an excellent cardiovascular exercise.

Rotating Knees

Begin in an upright stance. Now bend forward and hold both your knees with your hands. Slowly move both knees in a circular motion, clockwise followed by anti-clockwise direction.

This exercise is useful for relieving knee pain and also helps in toning your legs. It should be repeated multiple times for the best results. However, be mindful of your posture and do not go too fast and sprain your knee.

Practicing the Lohan Pattern Exercises

As mentioned earlier, these patterns effectively enhance your physical strength and calm your mind. Try to practice them at least once a day for the best results.

Here is a sample workout plan:

Monday - Rotating Knees (20 times clockwise & anti-clockwise)

Tuesday – Deep knee bending (50 times)

Wednesday – Carrying Mountains (20 times each)

Thursday – Drawing Knife (15 times on both sides)

Friday - Dancing Crane (50 repetitions) & Pushing Mountains (25 times each arm).

Saturday – Big Windmill (25 times clockwise & anti-clockwise)

Sunday - Separating Water (100 repetitions)

If you follow this plan for a month, your physical and mental health will improve significantly. Make sure to avoid foods with preservatives and processed sugar during the course of Lohan Pattern exercises.

Once you get familiar with all of the exercises, aim to do at least a couple of repetitions of each one on a daily basis.

Finding a Kung Fu Master Trainer

Performing the exercises by yourself could be overwhelming. So, we suggest hiring a Kung Fu master trainer to guide you through the process. However, finding one could be tough and your best bet is to ask around or look for one online.

Alternatively, you can also check out a few videos on YouTube that teach these exercises in detail.

Lohan Pattern Exercises for Beginners

If you are a beginner, starting with an easy exercise like rotating your knees or arms is best. Start off slowly and gradually increase your speed over time until the movement becomes fluid.

Once you build up enough stamina for this pattern, move on to other patterns. Some of the more advanced exercises, such as drawing a knife and dancing with a crane, can take months before you get used to them. So be patient and don't rush through your workout plan.

Also, it is important to focus on getting the stance right rather than focusing on repetitions. A good stance is what provides support to your body and aids in strengthening the muscles evenly throughout.

Lohan Pattern Exercises for Weight Loss

If you are looking at these patterns from the perspective of losing weight, then you're better off starting with the deep knee bend. This is because of its high intensity and will help you lose weight faster than other exercises.

However, it is suggested that beginners start small if they are not used to such strenuous activities. Rotating knees or arms is perfect for losing those extra pounds.

The Lohan Pattern is a series of exercises that are designed to have both physical and mental benefits. These exercises can do wonders from helping with weight loss, improving posture, alleviating joint pain, or just providing you with the opportunity for some deep breathing. However, they're not exactly easy. Start off slowly and take your time mastering each pattern before moving on to more difficult ones like drawing knives or dancing cranes. Also, remember to focus on getting the stance right instead of focusing solely on repetitions when performing these patterns. A good stance will provide support for your body and help strengthen all your muscles if done correctly.

Though all of these exercises look simple to perform, they are not easy. It takes a lot of focus and patience to perfect each movement pattern. So, we suggest that you don't rush through your routine and spend at least 15 minutes every day on Lohan Pattern exercises if you want the best results.

Chapter 6: Chi and Zen in Kung Fu

When practicing Shaolin Kung Fu, it is essential to keep in mind that there's more to it than just the physical aspect of the martial art. It also encourages practitioners to grow spiritually alongside their improvement in combat, and it does so by focusing on two concepts, Chi and Zen.

Understanding Chi

Chi, sometimes known as Qi, is a Chinese word that can literally be translated to "vapor," "air," or "breath." More metaphorically, it is often translated as "vital energy," "material energy," "vital force," or simply "energy."

This concept is critical to a number of traditional Chinese beliefs and practices, including Taoism, traditional Chinese medicine, and Chinese martial arts, including Kung Fu.

A simple way to understand it is to look at how the word is written in Chinese. The symbol for "Chi" is a combination of two other Chinese symbols, those for "steam" and "rice."

When understood according to the way the word is written, Chi literally represents the steam rising from rice or, more accurately, the energy the rice is giving out.

In the more basic sense, that's precisely what Chi is. The energy or the life force that animates the world. It encompasses a variety of phenomena known to the Western world and represents the flow and vibrations happening continuously at the molecular, atomic, and sub-atomic levels of nature.

Though Chi is little understood – and even less accepted – in the modern Western world, a variety of other cultures has theorized the idea of a life force that flows through all living things. This life force is known as:

- Ki in Japan

- Prana or shakti in India

- Ka by ancient Egyptians

- The Great Spirit by Native Americans

- Pneuma by ancient Greeks

- Ashe in Hawaii

- Ha or mana by Native Hawaiians

Indeed, some theorists even equate Chi to the Christian understanding of the Holy Spirit.

Types of Chi

There are numerous different types of Chi/Qi, as identified by practitioners of traditional Chinese medicine. These include:

- **Yuan Qi**: The innate Chi that we're born with. It is also known as Ancestral Qi.

- **Heaven Qi or Tian Qi**: Made up of natural forces, including the rain and the sun.

- **Earth Qi, or Di Qi:** Affected by Heaven Qi. For example, too much sun leads to drought, while too little sun causes the plants to die.

- **Human Qi, or Ren Qi:** Affected by Earth Qi in the same way humans are affected by the earth.

- **Hou Tain Qi (also known as Postnatal Qi):** The Chi that you absorb from food, water, and air that you consume during your life.

- **Wei Qi (or Protective Qi):** The Chi that acts as a protective sheath around your body.

Additionally, each internal organ has its own Chi. Some of these include the spleen, the liver, the lungs, and the kidneys.

Taoist cosmology holds that there are two other important forms of Chi: Yin-Qi and Yang-Qi, primordial masculine and feminine energies flowing through the world.

On the other hand, the practice of Qigong often involves using both Heaven and Earth Qis, while Feng Shui is the balancing of all three – Heaven, Earth, and Human Qis.

Each type has its own effects and uses.

Feeling Chi

In Qigong and traditional Chinese medicine, balanced and free-flowing Chi results in good health. On the other hand, if you have stagnant or imbalanced Chi, you will suffer from the disease. This holds true at both the micro (human) and macro (ecosystem) levels. Imbalanced Chi can lead to issues in the natural world.

There are numerous ways to re-establish free-flowing Chi through your body, including through the practice of Qigong and Feng Shui. One of the abilities that helps with this is the ability to perceive the flow of Chi, both in you and in others (both animate and inanimate) around you.

It is essential to keep in mind that the ability to feel Chi is a skill, which means that some people are simply naturally more gifted at it than others. In fact, if you're skilled enough, you may even unknowingly perceive the Chi around you.

Consider this, have you ever spoken to someone and gotten a "bad vibe" from them? Or walked into a room and was able to tell things were tense? Both of these are essentially your ability to feel the Chi of the people and things around you manifesting themselves.

Aside from making you more perceptive, the smooth flow of Chi in your body also enhances creativity and stabilizes your mood. Furthermore, it helps you reach a higher state of consciousness.

Working with Chi

There are numerous ways to work with your Chi. Some common techniques include:

- **Acupuncture**: Acupuncture points can be used to redirect the flow of Chi through the meridians of your body. The meridians are the "strings" connecting acupuncture points and serving as the "passageways" through which energy flows through your body.

- **Qigong:** A system of body movements and poses that help with Kung Fu training and cultivates and balances your Chi. Tai Chi is closely associated with Qigong. It is an internal martial style that involves more complex movements that are choreographed with breathwork and can be used for self-defense. Many scholars consider Tai Chi to be a subset of Qigong rather than a different style altogether.

- **Yoga and Meditation:** This helps unify the body and the mind. Certain yoga poses can help in the accumulation and blockage of Chi, which is released when you exit the pose, allowing the gathered Chi to flow through your body. Meditation helps you focus so you can get rid of any other blockages hindering the flow of your Chi.

Chi Exercises

Here are two exercises you can use when working with your Chi:

Breathing Exercise

For this exercise:

- Find a comfortable position. It can be sitting, standing, or even lying down.

- Inhale through your nose and exhale through your mouth, extending the exhalation for as long as you can.

- Let your body inhale automatically. When the air enters your lungs through your nose, open your mouth and let it all out.

- Repeat for as long as possible. Aside from helping you with your Chi, this exercise can also help you catch your breath when you're feeling breathless and can even help boost your energy levels.

Ball of Energy

To activate the ball of energy you will be working with, you should:

- Rub your hands together vigorously.

- Bring your hands in front of your face, holding them in a relaxed prayer position. However, do not let them touch each other.

- Focus your energy on the center of your palms. You should start to feel a sensation similar to a magnetic force between your palms.

- Try to imagine this force or energy coalescing into a small ball of light energy between your palms.

Now, you can start working with the ball of energy. To do so, you will need to:

- Separate your hands slowly, and then close them again (without letting them touch). You should feel a slight resistance between your palms, kind of like two magnets are repelling each other.

- Repeat the step above so that you can get familiar with the feel of the energy.

- Once you're ready, practice throwing the ball of energy from one hand to the other, throwing with one hand and catching it with the other.

- While maintaining equal distance between your palms, try to rotate the ball between your hands.

Blending Chi

In the exercise, you will start to become aware of the forms of Chi that surround you and start understanding how you can blend them together harmoniously. To perform the exercise, you should:

- Stand with your knees slightly bent and your feet shoulder's width apart.

- Shift your weight to the balls of your feet, staying aware of your body's front side. Concentrate on the energy passing through your legs, chest, torso, the tops of your arms and hands, and face.

- After holding this position, shift your weight to your heels. Now it is time to concentrate on how your energy passes through the back of your body, from the back of your head to your arms and spine, all the way down to your legs.

Note: While you will start out holding this position and the one above for only about a minute, after practice, you should be able to hold it for up to 5 minutes at once.

- Repeat the steps above, this time focusing on the left and right of the body rather than the back and front.

- Repeat the first three steps carefully. Repeat them in a way that the motion is as invisible to the naked eye as possible. Instead, use your mind to move your weight while you feel your Chi flowing through the front and back of your body.

- Try feeling the way your Chi flows through the front and back of your body simultaneously, rather than differently.

Chi, Qigong, and Shaolin Kung Fu

There are two aspects in traditional Kung Fu: Neigong (the external, physical exercises) and Neijing (internal exercises focusing on the Chi).

Practicing Qigong and working with your Chi helps you improve your skills at Neijing. This, in turn, is used to gain an advantage when using martial art in combat. For example, you can use Neijing to collect the energy you possess and direct this energy into an opponent through the contact point on their body. This contact point is the only gateway through which you can conduct Neijing energies.

Without conscious control of your Chi, Neijing is difficult (if not impossible) to learn. Starting small with a few exercises will help you build up to a point where you can control Chi well enough to employ it in Shaolin Kung Fu.

Understanding Zen

Zen is the Japanese term for the Chinese word "Chan," which, in itself, is the Chinese pronunciation of the Sanskrit word "Dhyana" ("meditation"). It is a name given to a particular school of Mahayana Buddhism that developed in China during the Tang Dynasty, before traveling across East Asia to Japan. Before it spread to Japan, it was known as Chan Buddhism.

Zen Buddhism emphasizes the practices of meditation, rigorous self-restraint, and an exploration into the nature of the mind and the nature of things. This insight is meant to be expressed in daily life, especially as a way to benefit others.

Essentially, Zen Buddhism focuses less on doctrine and sutras and more on actual spiritual practice to better understand the self, the world around you, and Buddhism itself.

While it is undeniable that Zen Buddhism has been influential in the way the outside world views Buddhism as a religion – think of how the word "zen" is used today – this doesn't explain how it is relevant to Shaolin Kung Fu.

Zen and Shaolin Kung Fu

Shaolin Kung Fu is known as such because it was developed in China's famous Shaolin Temple. While Chinese martial arts existed before the development of Shaolin Kung Fu, the rise of the temple represented the first time one was institutionalized.

The Shaolin Temple was also home to the monk Bodhidharma, who is traditionally credited with spreading Chan Buddhism in China.

Legend holds that Bodhidharma first reached and requested entry to the Shaolin Temple about 30 years after it was founded. When he was denied, he climbed into the mountains and meditated in a cave for nine years before he was finally allowed entry.

In those nine years, Bodhidharma is said to have exercised as a way to stay fit. These exercises were what would become the foundation for Shaolin Kung Fu. Thus, he is credited with being the creator of Shaolin Kung Fu.

While there are questions about the credibility of this story, it cannot be denied that the Shaolin Temple was both the center of Chan (or Zen) Buddhism and Kung Fu.

In 618, monks from the Shaolin Temple took part in battles to defend the Tang Dynasty, and in the 16th century, they defended the Japanese coastline from pirates and fought bandit armies.

Due to this link, Shaolin Kung Fu has long been generally considered a form of practicing Chan Buddhism and Zen. In fact, it was given the term "wuchan," or "martial chan," and was considered to be a form of inner cultivation in Chan Buddhism. Chinese Buddhism would later go on to adopt these cultivation exercises as a way to increase concentration. Indeed, in some ways, Shaolin Kung Fu can be considered the physical path to achieving Zen.

Zen is considered as a way to distinguish Shaolin Kung Fu and other East Asian martial arts like Judo from other sports.

It provides Shaolin Kung Fu practitioners with the ability to understand themselves better, going as deep as the core of their minds. Every Kung Fu movement involves energy control and mental awareness, which is heightened through the practice of Zen.

In combination with Shaolin Kung Fu, Zen helps people live a balanced and positive life.

While the Shaolin Temple went into decline during the Qing Dynasty, it remains a practicing Buddhist temple where Shaolin Kung Fu is still taught. While many people believe that the Shaolin Kung Fu taught at the temple today is the original form, others claim that the original Shaolin Kung Fu was too powerful, so the monks switched to teaching a less aggressive version.

Whatever the truth, the Shaolin Temple serves not only as the birthplace of Shaolin Kung Fu but also as a reminder of how Zen and Kung Fu are intrinsically connected.

Finding and Mastering Zen in Your Daily Life

You do not have to be an expert at Shaolin Kung Fu to work on mastering Zen. In fact, you don't even need to take too much time out of your day to focus on it. Here are some simple ways you can find and master Zen in your daily life:

Breathe

Zen emphasizes finding the stillness and peace in your life. However, the chaos of the day can often lead to worry, which is not conducive to finding peace.

One simple way to bring yourself back into balance is to take the time to breathe deeply. This doesn't have to take too much time. The next time you find yourself spiraling, take a time out and breathe deeply for a few moments. With each breath, breathe calmness in and breathe your worries out. You will be stunned at how effective this can be.

Close Your Eyes

Closing your eyes as a way to drown out the world may sound like a cliché, but it can actually work.

If you're feeling overwhelmed by life, take a moment to stop, lean back, and close your eyes. Focus on your inner self, not the chaos of the outside world, and appreciate the sense of stillness it brings.

If you've never done this before, you may have to build up your abilities slowly. You may notice that intrusive thoughts start to creep back into your mind after a few moments of stillness when you first start.

However, keep focusing inward when necessary, and you will soon find that you're able to revel in the stillness of your inner world for longer each time.

Take a Pause and Meditate

You don't need to have hours of free time in order to meditate. Five minutes between tasks will do just fine.

Here's how you can hold a mini-meditation session in the middle of your office:

- Sit in a comfortable position.

- Close your eyes

- Take deep, full breaths in and out. Breathe through your nose.

- Repeat the last step while observing your thoughts. Do not focus too much on what you are thinking, as that can distract you. Instead, just watch your thoughts go by, like cars on a highway.

Admit How You Feel

Many of us try to use the stress and chaos of everyday life as a way to escape challenging, difficult, and inconvenient feelings. However, denial only serves to exacerbate your inner restlessness and strife.

It is important to be honest and admit what you're feeling, even if it is only to yourself. If you're not ready to talk to a trusted friend, your partner, or a therapist, writing down your feelings in a journal or talking aloud to yourself can help.

Remember to be compassionate and non-judgmental when you acknowledge what you feel. Self-deprecation will only make things worse.

For example, if you're worried about an upcoming job interview, it is important to:

- Acknowledge that you're worried.

- Stay confident without denigrating yourself for being worried. Saying or thinking things like "I'm so stupid for worrying," or "I'm not qualified, of course, I will not get the job" will only make your inner strife worse. Instead, consciously try to shift your thought patterns to compassionate ones, like "Being worried is understandable, but I'm confident I'll do well," or "There's no reason for me to worry. I'm qualified and know my stuff inside and out."

Let Go

Holding on to thoughts, worries, and really anything negative whatsoever can not only lead to physical and mental clutter in your life, but it can also make it difficult for you to appreciate the here and now. While it isn't possible for us to simply let go of everything, practice it as much as we can.

Take a moment to clear out your workspace and discard items you no longer need or journal your thoughts so that you can move past them and leave them behind in the past. Declutter both materially and mentally as much as possible.

Now that you understand the importance of Chi and Zen in Kung Fu, it is also important to keep in mind that Kung Fu focuses on both the spiritual and the physical. Chi and Zen help you understand the value of the spiritual aspects of Kung Fu, but there's more to it than just the spiritual.

In the next chapter, you will move back to the physical aspects of martial art once more and look at the 18 weapons of Kung Fu.

Chapter 7: Weapons of Kung Fu

While many types of martial arts consider the body itself to be a weapon, in Kung Fu, actual weapons are simply extensions of your body. You need to be able to use them well to master Shaolin art effectively. It takes a particular set of physical and mental skills to imagine, believe, and accept a weapon as a part of your body. Methodically swinging a heavy broadsword should be as easy as gracefully deflecting a blow with Crane's Beak. Perfectly handling a staff needs to be second nature to you.

Years of training and practice go into mastering the numerous Kung Fu body forms, techniques, and katas, but it may take you several more years to become proficient in using weaponry. That is because there aren't just one or two swords or staffs to practice with but 18 different weapons that are believed to be sacred in the world of Shaolin, alternatively called the Eighteen Arms of Wushu. However, once you can combat and defend with each one expertly, you can protect yourself against any type of weapon.

Here, we will guide you through the nature, use, combative abilities, and defensive purposes of each of the 18 sacred weapons in Kung Fu. However, be very careful while handling those. Each weapon is insanely powerful yet extremely secure in the hands of a Shaolin master, but it can be equally dangerous for both the wielder and the opponent if used by an amateur. That said, you can't just magically master Kung Fu weaponry, so don't forget to practice with each weapon every day in a carefully controlled, safe environment.

1. Staff

Four weapons are revered more than the remaining 14. Those are the Straight Sword, Broadsword, Staff, and the Spear. The Staff is the most fundamental, highly reputable piece of them all. It is the "chief/father of weapons." There are several different types of Staff used in Kung Fu. To name a few, there is the khakkhara with an artistically designed top edge, the gun, which is a regular lean staff with a slightly broader hold, and the three-section staff that consists of three strong sticks connected with ropes or metal rings. Of these, the gun or the Bo is ideal for training purposes.

The Bo Staff is usually made out of wood, and it is best used for both offensive and defensive purposes. While it may look much like a snooker cue stick, it is not held in the same way. You need to grab it with both palms, face-up from the underside, and practice your moves from there. Being a long-range melee weapon, the gun has an exceptional reach in combat, and it can easily fend off most other Shaolin weapons. Balance is the key to mastering the art of Kung Fu, but you need a tad bit more of it to handle the Staff properly.

2. Straight Sword

Who doesn't love the look and feel of the Straight Sword? After all, it was the weapon of choice of many of our childhood heroes, mythical or real. It is not without good reason that the Shaolin Straight Sword is called "the gentleman," for it is indeed the weapon preferred by the admirably gentle yet extraordinarily valorous individuals. For the past 2500 years, Chinese Kung Fu specialists have used a double-edged Straight Sword (called jian), but you are free to practice with a single-edged one as well.

The jian may look like a ninjaken or a katana from afar, but the differences between the legendary Japanese ninja weapons and their Shaolin counterpart are starkly apparent up close. For one, the jian has a longer and wider hilt to protect your palms better from the opponent's sword. Secondly, double-edged Shaolin Straight Swords are more popular, unlike the single-edged ones preferred by the Japanese.

Many martial artists believe that the jian is the only weapon through which they can express their unique Kung Fu style. Its blade is generally forged from steel with a special technique called sanmei. It involves sandwiching a hard steel plate between two relatively softer ones. However, if you are a to-dai or a beginner in Kung Fu, then you will start off with a wooden Straight Sword with blunt edges.

3. Broadsword

A Broadsword is heavier than a Straight Sword but can be easily held in one hand. A Chinese Broadsword is nothing like those in Arthurian legends. Its blade grows wider from the hilt before curving at the top. Forged with a single-edge, it is referred to as dao in Shaolin culture. It comes in many different lengths, but Kung Fu masters believe that your chosen sword should reach your eyebrow when it is held vertically in your palm, pointing toward your face.

Of all the Eighteen Arms of Wushu, the dao is the "marshal" or the "general," implying that it assembles and leads all the other swords into battle. Regular Chinese Broadswords have a wider blade, but there are also daos with a small width, alternatively called sabers. The Broadsword is primarily an offensive weapon, most used for slashing and chopping actions. The hilt is curved in the opposite direction to the blade, maximizing the thrust of your cut.

The dao was once the most used weapon in the Chinese military, for it took only about a week to master its basics. Don't get your hopes up too high, though. Read that sentence again. *A week to master its basics.* Kung Fu is an advanced martial art, and it may take you several months, or even years, to effectively use the dao for offensive purposes.

4. Spear

The Kung Fu Spear may look and sound like an ordinary weapon, neither a full Staff nor a complete Sword, but its use in Shaolin is extraordinary. It is not without good reason that the qiang (Chinese name of the Spear) is called the "king" of all the Eighteen Arms. It has a leaf-shaped blade affixed on top of regular staff, giving it unparalleled reach in one-to-one combat.

Unlike the Chinese Sword, which features a tassel wrapped around its pommel, the qiang has one tied just below the blade. The color of that tassel denotes the rank of the infantry, and it is best used to distract the opponent in fast-moving, close-quarters combat. It is also ideal for absorbing and stopping the blood flowing down the handle, thus keeping it clean.

At Kung Fu training centers, the qiang is among the first weapons taught to the to-dai, for it is the perfect piece to learn the weaponized extensions of various Shaolin styles. The edges during training are blunt, and the handles are furnished out of wax wood to improve performance. Its length may vary, right from nine feet to over 21 feet, depending on the handler's height and capability.

5. Kwan Dao

As you may have guessed from the name, kwan dao, often stylized as guandao, is a lengthier version of the dao (Broadsword). The blade's width is more pronounced to maintain a healthy balance with the long handle, but its shape is almost the same as that of the dao.

The kwan dao is also akin to the Spear (dao blade fitted atop a long wooden pole), only the former's handle is usually carved out of metal, and its blade is more like a Broadsword than a knife. The sharp bend at the top of the blade coupled with its long reach makes the guandao exceptional for locking the opponent's weapon down, effectively parrying their attacks.

6. Pu Dao

The pu dao is almost exactly the same as the kwan dao, the only difference being that its handle is usually shorter than that of the latter. The remaining structure, down to the blade's curvature and its use in parrying and defending attacks, is the same as that of the guandao.

7. Shaolin Fork

Alternatively called a Tiger Fork or a Trident, the Shaolin Fork is used just like any long-range Wushu weapon. A three-pronged steel fork is attached to a metal staff, and a tassel is usually wrapped just below the trident to confuse the opponent. Quite a few of its Kung Fu styles are similar to the Spear and the kwan dao, but its techniques vary in many other forms and katas. The Shaolin Fork is perfect to set up a counter-attack in long-range melee fights.

8. Tri-Point Double-Edged Sword

From afar, the Tri-Point Double-Edged Sword can be easily mistaken for a Shaolin Fork, but upon taking a closer look, you can clearly notice the differences between the two. If you are an artist at heart, you will immediately realize that the blades in the Tri-Point are shaped like a lotus, with two side curvatures bending outward and the one in the middle shooting upward. The rest of its structure, right down to the material used, is similar to the Fork. It is typically used in parry-and-thrust styles of combat.

9. Ax

There is nothing different between a woodcutter's ax and a Wushu Axe. A wooden handle latched onto a solid, curved steel pane makes any kind of ax deadly in the hands of a Shaolin monk. Its Kung Fu variants usually include the varying length of the handle and the material used to forge it. Sometimes, you may also come across a double-edged Axe with a sharp peak, just like a Tri-Point.

Hacking and slashing is the main purpose of the Axe in Kung Fu, but it is often done with artistic grace, conforming to the pre-existing styles of the combat form.

10. Monk's Spade

A Wushu defensive weapon similar to the Fork but greatly varies in its practice styles. The Monk's Spade is twice as heavy as the dao, which brings the strength factor of the martial artist into the equation. While any to-dai can train with a wooden Shaolin Spade in a dojo, very few can actually use a real one in combat. It consists of a crescent-shaped blade affixed to a long pole, with the other end metal-forged like a spade. Given the blade's sharpness and curvature, it is mostly used for defensive moves and for maiming the opponent without inflicting any fatal injuries.

11. Da Mo Cane

Also known as the Bodhidharma Cane after the founder of Kung Fu and Zen, the Da Mo Cane is one of the most ancient weapons in the art of Shaolin defense. Shaped like a typical cane with no sharp edges, it is ideal for learning the Tiger Claw Wushu technique. Simply pick a Da Mo Cane based on your height so that it is well-suited for treading mountain paths, and begin your defensive katas in sync with the basic blocking and parrying stances.

12. Nine Section Whip

Simply called a Chain Whip. Its name was modified to the Nine Section Whip to denote the number of chain sections it contains. There may be fewer or more sections in different Chain Whips, and they are named accordingly. The Nine Section variant has been in use in Chinese martial arts for generations. In fact, in the earliest Wushu period, only the Seven Section and Nine Section Whips were available, but today, you can find ones with up to 13 sections.

Each segment of the chain is made from stainless steel. There is a wooden handle at one end and a metal dart at the other. The Nine Section Whip is widely considered to be the hardest weapon to master. You should be able to twirl and lash it around in quick motions, so much so that the dart becomes an invisible blur.

13. Hand Dart

A Shaolin Hand Dart is longer and heavier than a regular Dartboard dart. A feather-light tassel is bound to the pointy end of the dart just so that it could better guide it through the wind. Traditionally made out of stone, it is currently forged from iron and steel. It is generally used as a long-range projectile to take down far-off targets.

14. Flying Dart

A Flying Dart is customarily lighter than a Hand Dart, and it is called so because it flies back into the attacker's hand. A long rope is tied to the blunt end of a metal dart, which allows the martial arts specialist to swing the weapon around as they please. An accomplished Flying Dart user can pierce the opponent from all sides, even from the back. This weapon and the Nine Section Whip are a part of the Rope Dart family of ancient Chinese weapons.

15. Iron Pen

Pick any item in your house that looks like a long, thin pen. That becomes your Iron Pen. It requires a delicate hold, and its complementary Kung Fu moves are also quite gentle and elegant. A typical Shaolin Iron Pen is usually much heavier and longer than a regular pen carved from brass. It is ideal for strengthening your fingertips with the Chin Na technique. If the tip is sharper and the grip in the middle is more pronounced, you can also use it for some offensive and defensive maneuvers.

16. Thorn

There really isn't much to say about the Thorn because the name speaks for itself. The Shaolin Thorn is like any other thorn, only longer and pricklier. Depending upon the user, it may or may not be laced with poison. It is generally a weapon of choice for female Kung Fu specialists, for they can easily hide the Thorn in their long hair or tie it up in a bun with it. The weapon is flung at the opponent with precision and the intent to draw blood and weaken the person. Don't mistake it for the African tribal thorn, which is pelted at the opponent through a thin, circular mouthpiece.

17. Iron Flute

The Iron Flute is just that, a flute made of iron. It can be played to whisper a sweet melody, helping you meditate and soothe your senses, calming your mind, and getting ready for the next session of Wushu katas. At the same time, the Iron Flute doubles up as a weapon that can be used the same way as the Iron Pen. That is primarily the reason why the Chinese don't prefer the wooden flute over the iron-made one. The latter may generate a better sound, but it cannot be used as an effective weapon.

18. Shaolin Sickles

Many of the ancient Chinese Kung Fu practitioners were farmers. Hence, they naturally transformed the sickle, one of the most commonly used farming tools, into a deadly Wushu weapon. Shaolin Sickles are normally wielded in pairs. They are made of solid iron with a curved top edge and another short curve sprouting from the bend. The latter is most important for defensive moves, locking the opponent's weapon away while aiming an offensive strike with the second Sickle.

As you may have guessed by now, most of the Eighteen Arms of Wushu are merely modified renditions of everyday working tools, except the four primary weapons, the Staff, the Straight Sword, the Broadsword, and the Spear. In essence, a vastly experienced martial arts master can use any available item as a weapon. So, if you do not have easy access to any of the 18 weapons, don't hesitate to pick any tool from your garage that resembles a weapon and practice your Kung Fu forms with it.

The ideal environment in which you can wield and practice each of those weapons is a dojo under the watchful eye of a Shifu.

However, if there isn't a dojo in your neighborhood and you are forced to practice at home, be sure to clear out your room of any delicate, breakable items, especially the TV set, lamps, chandelier, and vases. The basement would be perfect for weapons training, and if you have a spare room with minimal furniture, that's even better.

Chapter 8: Striking and Lama Pai Kung Fu

Lama Pai Kung Fu is one of the most sought-after Chinese martial arts involving animal-style strikes and precision techniques. Striking in Kung Fu is placed under the umbrella term "Lama Pai," which means Lion's Roar. The practice evolves from a Tibetan tradition and can be traced back to the Qing Dynasty. In fact, Hop Gar and Tibetan White Crane are the older versions of this martial art and are collectively known as Tibetan Lama Pai today. All the relative techniques, movements, and sub-categories of Lama Pai fall under one figure called "Sing Lung." In Lama Pai, the striking movements are inspired by the crane, and the grabbing techniques can be attributed to the ape.

The system is believed to have been devised by a monk called Dai Dat Lama, or Ah Dat-Ta. The monk explored and traveled across Qinghai and Tibet with his nomadic tribe to find peace and meditate in seclusion. Ah Dat-Ta found a secluded spot and resided among the mountains to study Buddhist writings and find inner peace. The monk also diligently practiced his martial art skills. One day, as his meditation was disturbed by a fight between a crane and an ape, he saw the scenario as an inspiration to devise a new martial art involving movements based on the crane and the ape.

Striking Fundamentals of Lama Pai

Typically, Ah Dat-Ta's martial art is based on some effective grabbing moves inspired by the ape and the white crane's vital point striking techniques. He witnessed the bird fighting for its life using its giant wings and pecking at the ape's weak points, whereas the ape resisted and fought back with his powerful hand movements and swings. With this, the typical Lama Pai system consists of eight elbow strikes, eight palm strikes, eight fist strikes, eight kicking techniques, eight stepping patterns, eight stances, eight clawing or seizing techniques, and eight finger strikes. This makes the martial art system a set of 8 striking with eight moves in each set.

The fighting pattern and techniques also incorporate traces of Shuai Jiao (Manchurian wrestling), Mongolian wrestling, Indian hand techniques, and long arm techniques. Several foot movements also steadily became a part of Lama Pai. Ideally, this martial art is limited to these eight parts of divisions and was never open for exploration or to be broadened by practitioners and masters of Kung Fu.

Different Striking Techniques

Several techniques related to striking in Lama Pai Kung Fu are important for beginners and professionals as well. Practitioners learn a variety of strikes that involve a lot of hand and elbow movements.

8 Fist Strikes - Kyuhn Faat

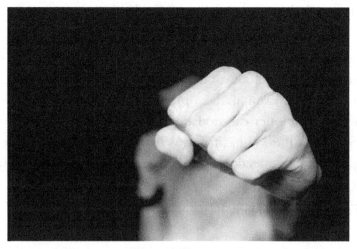

Photo by Dan Burton on Unsplash https://unsplash.com/photos/person-holding-persons-hand-nRW4I8kuyd8

Ideally, every fighter closes their hand to turn their fists into a weapon to attack or protect themselves. While the ancient Chinese developed their own form of using fists as self-defense, the ancient Greeks also devised another way to incorporate closed fists during the fighting. Among all martial art forms, Lama Pai particularly has a lot of fist strikes in a circular motion. The most basic forms of fist strikes are Uppercut - Paau Choih, Straight Punch - Chyuhn Choih, Horizontal Backfist (the thumb pointing towards the sky), Overhand Punch- Kahp Choih, Hook Punch- Gok Choih, Forearm Strike, Inward Sweeping Strike- So Choih, and 45 Degree Backfist Strike - Gwa Choih (the palm pointing towards the sky).

Some other forms of fist strikes include Chopping Fist - Pek Choih, Whip Strike - Bin Choih, and Small Trapping Strike - Siu Kau Dah. Even though fist strikes are powerful and act as strong, instant weapons, they need to be combined with other striking forms for effective results and to establish a strong attack and defense mechanism. Lama Pai also focuses on the principle of distributing the strikes among the upper and lower parts of the body, thereby improving the game. If the practitioner attacks the opponent's head multiple times, the rib cage is exposed, allowing them to attack their completely undefended legs.

When using the fist combinations in Lama Pai, the opponent takes continuous blows on their upper body, slowing them down and weakening their footwork. In turn, they are unable to use their hands and fists. Even if the opponent can intercept punches, a Lama Pai practitioner can dodge the moves by deploying the Right Side Stance or the Whip Strike. When combined with the Inward Swing Strike, the practitioner can attack and defend with maximum power.

8 Elbow Strikes - Jaang Faat

Jaang Fat

The eight most basic forms of elbow strikes are:

- Hyuhn Jaang (round elbow)
- Tai Jaang (upward elbow)
- Chum Jaang (downward elbow)
- Deng Jaang (straight elbow)
- Kahp Jaang (overhand elbow)
- Bong Jaang (inverse rising elbow)
- Bui Jaang (elbow to the rear)
- Bouh Jaang (folding elbow)

Some can be used independently, whereas others need to be incorporated with other techniques to form effective combinations.

8 Palm Strikes – Jeung

Jeung

The eight most basic forms of palm strikes are Twin Pushing Palms, Shoveling Palm, Chopping Palm, Single Thrust Palm, Groin Striking Palm, Propping Palm, Stamping Palm, and Slicing Palm.

The palms and claws are the strongest weapons in Lama Pai as they can be extremely versatile. When you keep an open hand, your fighting power gets stronger as it can be difficult to break an open hand. Unlike a closed fist, an open hand can make several movements and swing around multiple directions, thereby making palm and claw strikes more effective than fist strikes (not necessarily in every case but in most cases).

An open palm gives the fighter two ways to combat: the palm face and the edge (primary striking surfaces). When used in a circular or chopping motion, you can attack the opponent's upper body, specifically areas like the collar bone, the neck, the underarm, and the floating ribs. Edges of the palms can also be deployed in a thrusting motion. The face of the palm can cover larger parts of the upper body and face. Some fighters cup their ears using their palm's faces. In some cases, you can also use the palms to create space by pushing your opponent and causing them to lose balance.

8 Clawing or Seizing Techniques – Jau

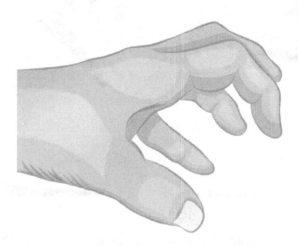

Jau

The eight most basic forms of clawing strikes are Single Tiger Climbs the Mountain, Upward Arm Seizing Claws, Crane Claw, Twin Downward Claws, Greater Trapping Claw, Lesser Trapping Claw, Bodhisattva Subdues a Tiger, and Inward Sweeping Grab.

Like the fists and the palms, a fighter can use their claws to grab or seize the opponent. Claws act as pulling weapons used to create imbalance and defend yourself from oncoming attacks and strikes. You can use your claws to pull, press, and twist the opponent's muscles and skin, thereby inflicting pain and distracting them.

8 Finger Strikes - Jih

The eight most basic forms of finger strikes are Finger Spear to Eyes, Crane's Beak, Dragon's Head, Phoenix Eye, Slicing Fingers, Arrow Fingers, Thrusting Finger, and Needle Finger.

Finger strikes are another important part of hand movements in Lama Pai Kung Fu practices. It is necessary to build strength and resistance in the fingers to consistently use them in your Kung Fu practice. For this, learners develop the skill of "Biu Gung," which develops finger muscles and strengthens bones to keep them from breaking during attacks and heavy blows in fights. Practitioners use their fingers to fight some of the most delicate and trivial parts of the body, like the eyes and inner, soft parts of the body. Duhk Ngaan Jih refers to the fingers used to poison (attack) the eyes, and Biu Jih refers to the main thrusting or attacking fingers. At times, the thumbs and second knuckles are also used during fights.

8 Kicking Techniques

The eight most basic forms of kicking techniques are Front Heel Thrust, Back Kick, Side Kick, Hooking Sweep, Floor Sweep, Inside Crescent Kick, Tornado Kick, and Cross Kick.

8 Stepping Patterns

The eight most basic forms of stepping patterns are 7 Star Footwork, Plum Blossom Footwork, Baat Gwa Footwork, Meridian

Footwork, Bik Bouh, Shuffle, Stealing Step Footwork, and Leaping Retreat.

8 Stances

The eight most basic forms of stances are Drop Stance, Single-Leg Stance, Kneeling Stance, Cat Stance, Cross Stance, Horse Stance, Figure 8 Stance, and Bow Stance.

Lama Pai and the Importance of Self-Defense

Being a traditional martial art, Lama Pai is often questioned on its self-defense or counterattack capabilities. Since some skills focus just on attacking, the opponent can easily counterattack and win the game. Typically, many Kung Fu styles and techniques allow one arm to swing below the waist or behind the body, which leaves room for a counterattack. Unless the practitioner is experienced or extremely skilled, they must be aware of these stances and apply their techniques with precision to defend themselves. This is taken care of by Lama Pai Kung Fu techniques.

In this martial art, the practitioner automatically swings their lead hand, places it in front of their body, and swings it back to defend themselves. They strike with their rear hand. This form and technique can also be seen in Western boxing, part of which is instilled by Lama Pai. However, the practitioner may be perceived as an open target, and the lead hand movements may be mistaken for an opening. In reality, the lead hand movement deflects a blow or strike to the opponent and protects from an attack. With this, you can easily strike the opponent's control with your rear hand while defending yourself. In turn, you get complete control of the game.

Even though Lama Pai places great importance on self-defense and counterattacks, it also stresses the points where the participants must attack to control the situation and turn things in their favor.

Like a Western boxer, a Lama Pai practitioner brings his fists close to his upper body and face to attack the opponent while saving themselves from a counterattack. Western boxing and many modern martial art practices can learn valuable lessons from Lama Pai Kung Fu, especially those involving self-defense techniques. Since a Western boxer leaves a lot of vital points open to the opponent's attacks, Lama Pai can teach them effective ways to counterattack or defend themselves.

Three Forms or Categories of Lama Pai

These eight divisions were simplified into distinct categories or forms to understand and learn martial art with ease. These forms are "Dou Lo hands," "Maitreya hands" (Neih Lahk Sau), and "Flying crane hands" (Fei Hok Sau).

Dou Lo Hands

This moniker comes from an Indian indigenous plant with an interior soft as cotton and an exterior hard as a coconut. The hard shell protects the soft inner seeds. The form "Dou Lo Hands" does not necessarily focus on the outer or main aspects of Lama Dai but on the internal factors and teachings. The "vein changing skill" is an integral part of the striking system.

Maitreya Hands - Neih Lahk Sau

This form is an advanced version of the basic Lama Pai martial art and incorporates several new hand techniques to hold, seize, or twist the opponent's vital parts or arms. This skill needs a lot of practice and is named the "vein seizing hand," inspired by its original name.

Flying Crane Hands- Fei Hok Sau

Fei Hok Sau

This form primarily involves open hands and fist movements to attack the opponent at their weak or vital points. It mainly uses the fundamental levels of Lamai Pai and the striking techniques, along with evasive footwork and kicking techniques. It also involves a lot of hand strikes and circular movements to keep the opponent alert.

To date, Lama Pai, or Lion Roar's Kung Fu, is taught across China and some Eastern parts and gaining traction across the Western world. Over time, martial art has evolved as several masters stepped in to explore the skill. Buddhist guardians known as the Gam Gong (diamonds) and saints known as the Lo Han inspired many hand moves and strikes. After Lion Roar's Kung Fu turned into Lama Pai, it was gradually overtaken by the new form, and the fundamentals were taught only to curious or advanced learners. However, the eight fundamentals were carefully recorded by teachers in the past, which is how we know about Ah Dat-Ta's developed Kung Fu martial art system.

Chapter 9: Kicking in Kung Fu

Kicks are an important part of many martial arts techniques, particularly in Kung Fu. Even though kicks are usually the second line of defense in Kung Fu, they are still regarded as a useful tool. Due to the prevalence of hand techniques in Kung Fu martial arts, many people assume there are very few or no kicking techniques in Kung Fu. On the contrary, Shaolin Kung Fu specifically has about 36 kicking techniques, with more than one type of kick in each technique. Although basic Kung Fu training only covers five kicking methods, if you learn the fundamental principles of each technique, advanced techniques will become easier to master.

Kicks, however, aren't as commonly used as strikes in martial arts because of their innate weaknesses. Although your legs are supposed to have 70% power while your hands give 30%, there's also a greater risk when you use your legs to attack. There is a greater chance of losing your balance when you use kicking techniques than striking practices. Because kicking is a more difficult technique to learn and has numerous safety risks, it is critical to learn as much as possible about the various techniques before you start to learn.

The Characteristics of a Good Kick

Because of the many safety risks, kicking techniques are more difficult to master and require certain characteristics to be effective. A good kick should have the following characteristics.

1. Instinctive Accuracy

A good kick should be thrown accurately to hit the opponent correctly. As a martial arts practitioner, you should also be able to select the correct kicking technique based on the situation. Many factors affect this, including the spatial distance, exposed pain points, and how much damage you want to inflict. Your instincts should be able to predict which point you want to hit while also keeping in mind your own safety. For example, if you hit your opponent's bone with your toes, it would cause a severe fracture and render you unable to kick for a while, not to mention the immense pain it would cause.

2. Power

Although legs are said to exert more power than your arms, they can be completely useless if you don't know how to throw your power correctly. If your kick doesn't exert a specific amount of power on your opponent, it will be of no use, and your opponent will not suffer any damage. This is why it is important that you understand each technique and how to power your kicks precisely in order to induce maximum damage.

3. Speed

The speed with which you kick plays an important role in how effective your kicks are. If you keep your speed high, there will be fewer chances of being intercepted or dodged, whereas slower kicks will only make you vulnerable to attacks on the lower part of your body. Your opponent will easily be able to trip you if your kicking techniques are too slow, not to mention, the power wouldn't be maintained either. However, kicking fast is an advanced skill that requires hard work and practice, but your techniques will become infinitely better once learned. Make sure that you work on other skills, too, like power, balance, and instincts, because without them, speed will not do you much good.

4. Timing

Every fighting situation is different and requires a different time set to throw your kick accurately. First, you've got to identify if there is enough time to throw a kick without alerting the opponent of your move. Second, you will need to consider which kicking technique you can use in said time. When you time your kick correctly, the chances of it hitting your opponent effectively are increased. Otherwise, you can miss your target and make yourself susceptible to tripping or falling.

5. Muscle Chain

When you use the maximum number of your body's muscles to throw a kick, it can be infinitely more powerful than a regular kick. This is because utilizing the muscle chain reduces the chances of interrupting energy flow in your movements and will require considerably less effort than a normal kick.

6. Unpredictability

One of the most important characteristics of a good kick is its unpredictability. If your opponent is a good fighter, they will be easily able to identify your movements and either block or deflect your kick or attack your lower side to make you trip. This is why you should first learn every technique and apply these characteristics to improve your kick throwing skills significantly.

Basic Kicks

There are six basic types of kicks you need to learn about first if you want to understand the advanced kicking techniques in Kung Fu. If you understand the basic principles and movements of these types, it will be significantly easier for you to learn the complex techniques we'll discuss later on.

1. Back Kick

Back Kick

This is one of the most widely used kicking techniques across numerous martial arts. Back kicks are powerful and inflict maximum damage to your target. Follow these instructions to master your back kick.

- Use your rear leg for this technique, get into a kicking stance, and turn your body to the right until you are facing directly away from your target.

- Continue turning to your right while keeping an eye behind your right shoulder.

- Lift your right knee to your chest and drive back the heel of your foot straight to your opponent.

- After hitting your target, you quickly resume your kicking stance in a defensive position and get ready for the next kick.

2. Front Kick

Front kicks are simple, precise, and hit the target with maximum power to cause considerable damage. Front kicks usually involve hitting your target with the ball or heel of your foot. Follow these instructions to learn the front kicking technique.

- Raise your dominant leg's knee and thrust your foot forward

- Hit your opponent with the ball or heel of your foot - make sure to avoid hitting with your toes.

- Bend your toes upward prior to the kick to avoid any damage

- After hitting your target, withdraw your leg to avoid being grabbed or tripped.

Front Kick

3. Ax Kick

Ax kicks are used to target the opponent's head or clavicle. The following instructions will ensure that you correctly use this technique.

- Raise your rear leg (the dominant one) as high as you can in the vertical direction.

- Hit the target with the heel of your foot. The hard bone of your heel is more effective than striking with the ball of your foot.

- Target either the face or shoulder bone of your opponent to induce maximum damage.

- Be careful of your lower body, as this technique will leave it exposed to any attacks.

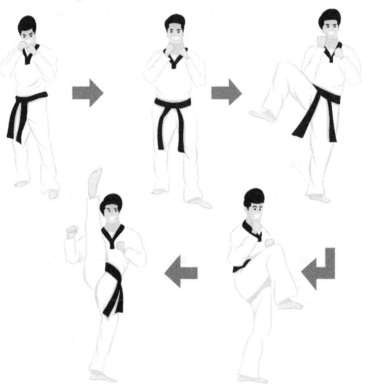

Ax Kick

4. Side Kick

Although sidekicks are considered to be powerful, they are much slower than the other techniques and leave your body wide open to counter attacks. This kick can be done using your rear leg or front leg and requires you to chamber in power before releasing your leg. Follow the instructions given below to ensure you can throw an effective sidekick.

- Rotate your body until it is at a 90-degree angle from your opponent

- Pivot 180 degrees on your front leg

- As you rotate, bring your rear leg forward until your knee is near your waist. Your foot should be facing the attacker.

- Your knee should be almost 270 degrees from the starting position if you want to launch your kick correctly.

- Thrust your foot forward and use the heel or blade (outer edge) of your foot to strike your target.

Side Kick

5. Roundhouse Kick

The roundhouse kicking technique is one of the most commonly used kicks and one of the easiest in martial arts. Also, unlike the other types, this technique doesn't focus on attacking a specific part of your opponent's body and can instead be used to target any part. Whether you want to attack your opponent's knee or chest, or head, you can power your kick accordingly and deliver an efficient and strong kick. The basic roundhouse kick can be mastered by practicing the following steps.

- Use your front or rear leg depending on your preference

- Get into your fighting stance by taking a big step forward with your left leg and letting your right leg naturally pivot towards the side

- Bring your leg up and bend it back upon itself so that it is touching the thigh.

- Bring your bent leg to the side so that your knee chambered

- Snap your leg forward and pivot on your lower foot - make sure you make contact with the target before your leg is fully extended for maximum effect.

- After hitting your target, retract your leg and get back into your fighting stance.

Roundhouse Kick

6. Crescent Kick

The crescent kick has many advanced techniques, but the most basic ones are the inside and outside crescent kick. Follow these steps to ensure you do it correctly.

- Bend your kicking leg similar to how it is done in a front kick.

- Point your knee deceptively towards the left or right point of the actual target.

- Whip your leg into an arc, and hit your target from the side

- According to the technique used, the arcing motion starts from the center of your body and moves outward or inward.

Crescent Kick

Advanced Kicks

Advanced kicking techniques are basically derived from the basic kicking techniques and should therefore be easier to master. Listed below are a few of the numerous advanced Kung Fu kicking techniques available. Follow the steps for each of the following, and practice on your own first before moving on to a real opponent.

1. Butterfly Kick

- Make sure you're facing the direction you want your kick to hit.

- Get into a forward bow stance by placing your legs apart and placing both your feet at 45 degrees.

- Extend your arms out to build momentum for your kick

- Lift your heels from the ground and pivot your feet 90 degrees

- Swing your arms to gain momentum

- Bend your body forward and pivot 180 degrees on one leg, then lift your leg and extend it behind you

- Jump off your other leg and pivot it to hit your target, and land back on this leg

Butterfly Kick

2. Cartwheel Kick

• Place your right foot behind your shoulder and shift your weight to the right.

• Raise your left forearm to defend your exposed area.

• Transfer your weight to the left and bend sideways, push into the floor with your left leg and hand

• Lift your right leg up and hit the target

Cartwheel Kick

3. Uppercut Back Kick

• Get into a fighting stance similar to the one in back kicks. Make sure you keep an eye on your opponent over your shoulder

• Raise your leg in your back until it reaches your thighs

• Use the heel of your foot to hit the pain points of your opponent

• Ensure you keep your hands in a protective stance to deflect counterattacks

Uppercut Back Kick

4. Spinning Hook Kick

• Get into a fighting stance with bent knees and legs far apart

• Swing your arms around with the non-kicking leg to build momentum for the kick

• Spin 180 degrees and look over your shoulder to gauge kicking power and distance

• Lift up your kicking leg and throw a hook kick to your opponent's chest or shoulder

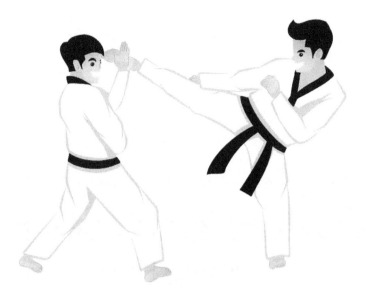

Spinning Hook Kick

Although practicing these kicks might seem like a harmless activity, you should make sure you get the guidance of a Kung Fu martial arts specialist. Plus, if you're trying these kicks on an opponent, make sure you don't exert damaging force onto your opponent's body as it can cause permanent damage. It is a good idea to first learn in detail the basic types of kicks before moving onto the advanced ones because the underlying principles remain the same throughout. You will find numerous advanced techniques, which will be almost impossible to master if you don't learn the basics of a good kick first. Practice makes perfect, and you should practice as much as you can if you want to master these kicking techniques to perfection.

Chapter 10: Self-Defense in Kung Fu

Kung Fu is much more than just a martial art. It is an art form that teaches us multiple life lessons. While many people assume that all martial arts are focused on attack, only a few are aware of the defensive aspect of these arts. Wing Chun is a truly unique style of Kung Fu that focuses primarily on defending oneself. It is a very intricate and beautiful style of Kung Fu that teaches a person the ability to defend themselves against almost every possible attack.

Wing Chun is so popular that it is a widely recognized sport in multiple parts of the world. There's a very logical reason behind this popularity, and it is the fact that Wing Chun is the most in line with today's needs. Martial arts aren't what they used to be because we live in a relatively safer society regulated by law. Since we don't need the lethal forms of martial arts in modern society, Wing Chun provides an excellent alternative to those who seek to learn self-defense.

The core elements of Wing Chun are simultaneous blocking and striking coupled with trapping the opponent, attacking from a close distance, pressurizing the opponent with movement, and a flurry of punches. Many more elements give Wing Chun its unique reputation, but these are the most well-known and visibly apparent characteristics. The unique quality of Wing Chun that separates it from other forms of martial arts or even Kung Fu is that it is especially effective when applied in a self-defense scenario. Perhaps, this is because Wing Chun can cripple an aggressor without lethally harming them. The ability to defend oneself while staying on the right side of the law is something that everyone wants, and that's where Wing Chun shines the most.

Wing Chun Today

Before we further explore how Wing Chun can help with self-defense, it is important to know a little bit about the current state of this martial art. Most of the training provided in Wing Chun by non-native masters are either focused solely on training or completely wrong. While it is perfectly fine to focus on training during the initial phases, Wing Chun is a practical art that must be regularly practiced.

Training can't provide the same level of experience and knowledge as practicing Wing Chun with a partner or in competitions. These unrealistic training methods have led to Wing Chun developing a much softer image than what it actually is. The extremely complex techniques each have their own merit, but not in the case of self-defense scenarios.

We'll be discussing many techniques that aren't as emphasized as some of the fancier ones because of aesthetic reasons only. These lesser-known techniques are in no way less effective than the ones being taught in almost every martial arts dojo. On the contrary, the techniques we'll discuss are some of the most important ones to learn from a self-defense standpoint.

Wing Chun has slowly been turned into an exercise in showmanship, and all the techniques and methods utilized are absolutely redundant in a real-world scenario. Problems like these usually arise because of the changing nature of Wing Chun. When we talk about Wing Chun as a self-defense martial art, we need to understand that it differs from the regular forms. However, the same can be said for every martial art that has both showmanship and self-defense applications.

Fundamentals of Self-Defense

1. Structure

Wing Chun is a martial art that's performed with a focus on offense as well as defense. The main goal of a Wing Chun practitioner is to trap, lock, or jam their opponent's limbs to create windows of attack. Not only does a Wing Chun practitioner need to develop their strength, but they also have to focus on developing their technique in a structured manner so that their strength is multiplied. All the different techniques fall under subgroups like punches, blocks, and kicks. If you can learn to use these techniques in conjunction with the forward motion aspect of Wing Chun, you will be able to overcome any opponent.

2. Offense vs. Defense

I have stressed this point many times in this chapter, but its significance requires that I repeat it again. Wing Chun is a Kung Fu style that demands symmetry between being offensive and defensive, which means that a strike will accompany every block you make. The same thing applies to strikes. You will learn to use different strikes to deflect attacks. This feature is only present in a few other martial arts like Muay Thai. The remainder of martial arts don't utilize this sophisticated style of fighting, and this is why Wing Chun is a lot more technical in nature. Practitioners will need to balance their offensive and defensive training at all stages of their development.

3. Trapping

Trapping is one of Wing Chun's aspects that declined in popularity due to poor teaching and practice methods. While the experts can utilize Wing Chun trapping to subdue an opponent effectively, the vast majority of practitioners have absolutely no clue how to do that. Due to a lack of regular practice and sparring, the fighters choose to rely on other more dominant aspects of Wing Chun. Because of this, most of the sports community believes Wing Chun sparring can't be applied in scenarios like an MMA fight or a self-defense scenario.

Trapping is something that every fighter should focus on. Knowledge of the various Wing Chun style traps will help amplify a practitioner's strength. However, it is important to understand that the fancier traps are nothing but a series of smaller traps layered on top of each other. They will never be as effective as the simpler, less flashy, and much more effective traps.

4. Sparring

Sparring is the eventuality that all practitioners of Wing Chun must face after they've been training for a while. No matter how much training you've done, you wouldn't be able to defend yourself against enemy attacks unless you practice all your moves in a real-life scenario. This is why sparring is such an important aspect of Wing Chun. It helps you push your boundaries with a partner without risking any fatal injuries.

The reason sparring is so effective is that the movements of your opponent are unpredictable. The proper way to spar is to do it lightly without any intentions of hurting your partner, more of a dance than a fight because you have to reciprocate with equal force. The major mistake made while sparring is that both the fighters practice their Wing Chun techniques. While this is perfectly fine from the competitive perspective, it will not be very useful in a street fight! One partner should ideally mimic the moves of an untrained fighter because it is highly unlikely that your opponent in real life will also be adept at Wing Chun.

Techniques of Wing Chun

Whenever a fighter, a warrior, or a soldier goes into battle, they have to bring the proper tools to fight. In the case of self-defense, your techniques are your tools. You should have perfect mastery over those to be able to defend yourself. Every fighter should have a variety of tools to counter the various situations they may find themselves in, and this is why you need to be an expert in multiple techniques.

In this section, we're going to explore the various techniques you should try to master for self-defense purposes. While the fancier moves are definitely a crowd-pleaser, our focus here is on efficiency and being able to defend yourself. This is why we'll only be looking at the essential techniques you should master first before moving on to more complex moves.

1. Hand Strikes

Hand strikes are some of the most important ones in any martial art because our hands are the most intuitive part of the body. Striking with hands isn't as emphasized in Wing Chun as blocking is, and that's primarily because of the defensive nature of martial art. However, these strikes play an important role nonetheless, and we'll be looking at some of the most important hand strikes you should learn.

Bin Sau: Also known as the Thrusting Fingers technique, Biu Sau simply involves darting your hand forward with tremendous force to damage the soft spots on your opponent's body. Remember that the fingers play a critical role here, and conditioning them properly should be your foremost priority.

Lin Wan Kuen: This isn't just a single strike like the previous attack. It is known as the Chain Punch due to the flurry of strikes that the practitioner must learn to throw. The main goal here is to overwhelm your opponent, and it is one of the most surprising attacks you can do to defend yourself.

Punches: This is a broader category than the previous two and involves multiple types of punches in Wing Chun. You should aim to practice the One-Inch Punch, the Double Punch, and a few other basic punches so that your arsenal isn't limited and, thus, predictable.

2. Kicks

Unlike kick-centric martial arts such as Tae Kwon Do, Wing Chun focuses more on upper body attacks and blocks. However, learning how to deliver a well-executed kick is still very important as kicks help increase your range and damage output. Every martial artist should know a few basic kicks like the Straight Kick, Side Kick, Hammer Kick, and Round Kick. You don't need to learn fancy kicks like the Roundhouse or the Tornado Kick for self-defense, as you will not have the time to use these in a real fight.

3. Elbow Strikes

Mostly associated with martial arts like Muay Thai, elbow strikes can be particularly devastating if executed properly. The biggest benefit of using elbow strikes is that you can surprise your opponent and deliver a lightning-fast blow that's almost guaranteed to cripple them for a brief moment. The most popular elbow strike in Wing Chun is the Pai Jarn, and it generally involves hitting the opponent's head to increase the amount of damage done.

4. Blocking

Blocking is one of the most significant aspects of Wing Chun, and an attack usually accompanies the blocks executed by a Wing Chun fighter. This means that you can deal massive damage while reducing the chances of you getting hurt in the process.

Biu Sau: We discussed Biu Sau in the hand strikes, and it is a highly versatile move that can be used to divert, attack, and counter-attack at the same time.

Chi Sau: Also known as the Sticking Hands technique, Chi Su involves rapid hand movements supported by the executor's reflexes and speed. You can easily and rapidly deflect a flurry of attacks from your enemy by utilizing this technique which will provide you with ample openings to strike the enemy.

Huen Sau: This technique is sometimes also referred to as the Circling Hands technique, and it is very useful if you want to change positions while still retaining control over an opponent's arm.

Kwan Sau: The Rotating Hand technique is most useful when you want to block simultaneous low-level and high-level attacks from your enemy. Your opponent will often try to overwhelm you with such attacks in a real fight, and when you execute this block, you will be able to nullify them entirely.

Pak Sau: This technique is also known as the Slapping Hand Block, and it is very useful if you need to deflect an incoming attack with ease. This involves utilizing your palm to deflect the attack, and it can even divert the direction of attack, which can cause your opponent to lose their balance.

Chapter 11: Daily Training Drills

Having covered all of the different techniques, styles, and exercises that go into creating a well-rounded Kung Fu routine, as with many other things in life, practice makes perfect. Even simple routines such as basic strikes and kicks need to be thoroughly practiced if you want to gain mastery of these moves and take your Kung Fu to the next level.

Without regular practice and proper focus on improving your skillset, it will be close to impossible to improve as a martial artist. Whether you are a complete beginner who has only learned the basics or someone more advanced learning the more technical moves, it always requires constant work. Martial arts relies on you knowing about the move and theoretically understanding the concept and shifting that knowledge and applying it to your body, and teaching it to move in a certain way. Just like boxing, mixed martial arts, and any other kind of physical activity, repetition will burn this information into your muscle memory and hardwire it into your nervous system. This is crucial when it comes to really perfecting a move. More importantly, when you need to use one of these moves in a match or even in everyday life, you will not have the time to think about it. You need to be able to react quickly and efficiently.

If you look at professional football players, you will see that they practice the same routine hundreds of times throughout the year, during training and competition seasons. This way, when they are actually in a match, they don't have to do any thinking since their bodies already know what needs to be done. This applies to nearly every sport and is an effective solution for both game strategy and specific moves that a player uses.

It is no different in Kung Fu. As you progress, you learn more complex skills, and your muscle memory becomes even more important. You don't want to learn new things at the expense of older and often more fundamental skills. Staying in touch with basic movements will also keep your body nimble and ready to absorb more advanced skills that build on those basic movements.

If you have the time to enroll in a martial arts academy, you should definitely do that. You will not only be training in the things you need, but you will also have the chance to immerse yourself in a great atmosphere and be surrounded by like-minded people. You will have access to lots of equipment and skilled teachers who will be vital in improving your practice sessions. However, don't let your lack of resources or time limit your Kung Fu training. Even if you are on your own and don't have any equipment to train with, you can get in a very good session that will help both your physical fitness and your Kung Fu.

However, if you really want to be self-sufficient, you should definitely consider getting some basic equipment. This doesn't have to be extremely expensive. In fact, most of the basic equipment you need can be quite cheap. For instance, a medium-sized wooden dummy, a few stretching bands, and some basic resistance equipment are not very expensive and portable. You can easily take these things with you if you need to be out and about frequently. These items are also very easy to manage and store at home. If you are serious about developing your Kung Fu, good equipment is a must-have.

To make daily training a bit more manageable, let's look at some specific things you can do to improve particular aspects along with some holistic training routines you can use.

Stretching

Kevin Poh, CC BY 2.0 <https://creativecommons.org/licenses/by/2.0>, via Wikimedia Commons https://commons.wikimedia.org/wiki/File:Shaolin_Kung_Fu.jpg

This is a critical part of any good training routine and important if you want to perform moves properly. Nearly every kind of move you come across, whether a flip, kick, or punch, will require you to have solid joints and the ability to fully and properly extend your limbs and torso. Even simple breathing techniques require you to fully expand and contract your entire torso so you can get the maximum amount of oxygen into your system and generate the maximum amount of force in strikes. Similarly, flexibility in the hips, lower back, and waist are extremely important for martial arts. Whether you are punching, kicking, dodging, or doing anything else, this central part of your body is what allows you to generate momentum.

Any stretching routine you do should incorporate a portion, especially for your core and the rest of your spinal column. It is also important that when you are stretching at the start of the workout, you take it nice and slow and don't force any fast or explosive movements. You can incorporate stretching as part of your warm-up routine, or you can do it separately, where you focus on certain areas of your body that feel tight. Ideally, you should have a bit of both where stretching is part of your warm-up and cool-down routine. You also have a separate time when you only focus on stretching and flexibility.

Warm-Up

Benjamin Korankye, CC BY-SA 4.0 <https://creativecommons.org/licenses/by-sa/4.0>, via Wikimedia Commons https://commons.wikimedia.org/wiki/File:Emp_Qorankye.jpg

If you ask any seasoned martial artist what the key to a healthy and sustainable routine is, they will tell you it is proper body management, and this starts with the warm-up. You can easily avoid many problems and significantly reduce your chances of injury if you just spend an extra ten minutes before the workout properly warming up and a few extra minutes after the training to cool down properly. Warm-up routines don't have to be related to your martial arts training, and you can do anything like going for a walk or swimming or jogging or even just doing some cardio to warm up. In fact, the Shaolin monks and many other eastern martial artists always start off their day and their training with a run.

This could be a short 10-minute run or even a thirty-minute run, but the point is that it serves as a gentle warm-up that gets the entire body ready for a workout. If you have a treadmill at home, that's fantastic. If you don't, just go for a little walk outside and get yourself properly warmed up before you start training. If you are about to do some explosive movements, getting warmed up is key. Similarly, warming up is about your cardiovascular system just as much as it is about getting good blood flow to your muscles. With both areas properly warmed up, you are ready to train.

Combat

Photo by SOON SANTOS on Unsplash https://unsplash.com/photos/men-doing-karate-in-park–XGqShGxO8E

Essentially, the purpose of all the intense Kung Fu training is to make you a better fighter and to give you all the skills and knowledge you need to construct a better fight routine. However, even with the different skills, there are a variety of ways to apply them. Using the various combat styles such as the Tiger style, Dragon style, Praying Mantis style, Leopard style, and others, you can better perform your skills and take down your opponent more efficiently. These different kinds of combat techniques involve their own unique moves and strategies. If you want to really master a certain style, you need to learn the minor variations of each one.

The small differences, such as the slight variation in the way the hand is held between the Dragon style and the Tiger style, can have a big impact on how the move is executed. More importantly, the different styles also influence your overall combat strategy. While some styles such as the Tiger style are more aggressive and require you to be more offensive other styles such as the Dragon style will allow you to be more elusive and strike more strategically.

Also, the kind of style you wish to pursue will also have a big impact on the kind of training you do and how you build up your body to support a certain fighting style. For instance, if you wish to pursue the Tiger combat style, there will be a higher focus on physical fitness. It requires more calisthenics, and there is a greater importance on sparring instead of just perfecting moves.

Striking

Photo by Uriel Soberanes on Unsplash https://unsplash.com/photos/man-doing-karate-stunts-on-gym-ngd2uo1eyZg

In any kind of martial art, the purpose is self-preservation. You are trying to protect yourself from an attacker. To do this effectively, you need to be able to strike with power, accuracy, and speed.

Without a good combination of these three factors, you may still fight, but your attempt to stop the attacker will not be effective, and they will continue to attack while you continue to run out of energy and eventually get defeated.

When you practice striking, you want to make sure that you are unleashing a good strike. This means that your strike is quick, powerful, and targets the right areas. If you are about to launch a very complex attack, but you don't have sufficient power behind it, or your strategy is not good enough to break through the opponent's defense, the complexity is of no use.

When striking, the first thing to consider is your stance, the base from which you launch the attack. You need to be in a good position, and you need to learn how to efficiently position yourself in the ring or wherever you are to formulate a good attack. The most important things in a good stance are the position of your feet and the equal distribution of weight.

Next, you need to be aware of your distance from the opponent. Whether you are using your hands and legs for punches and kicks or using a weapon, having the right range of motion will help you get the most out of the strike. If your opponent is too far or too close, it will undermine the amount of power you can generate, and you might not even be able to land the shot where you want to. So be aware of your distance from the opponent at all times.

A good strike has to take the quickest route and be a rapid movement. There is no need for a big flowing movement when you want to land a reverse heel kick - more movement reduces efficiency. To make the strike hit hard, it must be fast, and it must have excellent momentum from the launch to the final point of impact. Also, you want to make sure you are using your Chi to drive additional energy into the strike. Keep things simple and be quick in your movements to generate as much force as possible.

Whether you use a weapon or your hand, you want to be able to put as much mass into the move as possible. This means incorporating your entire body into the movement. Mass combined with speed creates power, and when you put your entire body into the movement, you increase mass exponentially. Be very careful which direction your body is moving in when launching an attack, and try to streamline your entire body to create a solid strike.

Another great way to add momentum and force to your strike is with rotation. Spinning on your heels, spinning from the waist, or simply shifting the weight from one foot to another is a great way to make use of torque. What you want to eliminate is counter-rotation, as this reduces momentum and slows down the movement.

When launching a strike, you also need to pay extra attention to the angle from which you are launching it and the angle at which the strike will land on the opponent. This can often be the difference between a strike that has a very small impact and one that ends the match. Understand where you are hitting the opponent and what kind of angle is most effective for that area, then change your attack angle accordingly.

Kicking

Photo by Thao LEE on Unsplash https://unsplash.com/photos/man-wearing-karate-gi-standing-on-road-UpFy6jbnXS4

You can use countless kicks in Kung Fu to defend yourself, but generally speaking, these can be categorized as forward-thrusting kicks, lifting kicks, and spinning kicks. Moreover, other kicks can be used for close-range or long-range fights, but they too will be based on either a thrust, a lift, or a spin. Ideally, you want to be proficient in a wide variety of kicks. Kicks help keep a distance from the opponent and create a lot more force than what you would be able to with a punch.

Self-Defense

Photo by SOON SANTOS on Unsplash https://unsplash.com/photos/two-men-about-to-sparring-sab37qbGmHc

If your aim is self-defense, then Kung Fu is something that can come in handy. It originated on the battlefield as a form of fighting that will incapacitate an opponent with many kinds of strikes that can be fatal when done right. To make your Kung Fu lethal, you don't need to know very advanced skills, but you do need to be extremely proficient in the execution of basic skills. However, as important as attacking is, it is also important to be very proficient in defensive techniques and dodging techniques to protect yourself properly. With the right combination of defense and attack, you can outplay any opponent. Relying on just one of these two things will not help you in most situations.

General Kung Fu Workout Ideas

Photo by RDNE Stock project https://www.pexels.com/photo/shirtless-man-kicking-a-punching-bag-7187986/

As you can tell, a good Kung Fu routine addresses a lot of things and one in which training is balanced. You need a good mix of everything to have a solid foundation in Kung Fu that you can use to learn more advanced skills. To this end, there are a lot of masters and even grandmasters who still practice very basic training every single day. The fact is that these basic things are taught to new fighters not because they are simple but because they are the foundation. The horse stance is a perfect example of something so important in so many ways. Simply holding the horse stance every day for thirty minutes is a fantastic exercise.

However, you can also use some general workout principles to help you train more effectively.

Warm-up – 15 minutes of running or jump rope or 30 minutes of walking.

Workout

- 4-second stretch (4 times per side)

- 2-second stretch (4 times per side)

- leg swings (10 times on each leg, both to the front and to the side)

- low kicks (5 times on each leg)

- 9-count pushups (a minimum of 10 or as many as you can do)

- knuckle pushups (however many your target does it in one set)

- sit-ups (again, do your daily target in one set)

- Horse stance (start by holding the position for 1 minute and increasing it by 30 seconds each week. Beginners should aim for a total time of 5 minutes, intermediate students 10 minutes, and advanced students 20 minutes)

- hamstring stretch, straddle stretch, butterfly stretch, dragon drop stretch, twist stretch (2 minutes each, total 10 minutes)

This is a sample workout that you can easily do every day, as it doesn't require a lot of equipment, it is quick, and it is effective. Of course, if you have a certain kind of training that you are focusing on, you can carve out a routine that better addresses that. However, as a daily training routine, you want something that will work on your overall strength, flexibility, and the basic requirements for Kung Fu movements.

Conclusion

In this ultimate guide to Kung Fu, we have provided a comprehensive and practical look into this type of martial art. The book covers critical elements of Kung Fu like stances, different patterns, weapons, self-dense, and daily training drills. You need to understand how to execute different moves against the opponent before you actually employ any of the moves for self-defense. Read this book to learn a step-by-step approach to this amazing martial art.

Many people have heard of Kung Fu, and some believe that it is an exceptional art for highly talented and skilled individuals. However, with the appropriate knowledge under your belt, you can also become proficient in this form of martial art. This book offers you the information on critical techniques and stances you need to understand how to overcome opponents. It also explains how Kung Fu differs from other types of martial arts.

If you are interested in developing your knowledge and skills in Kung Fu, it is vital to know where it is similar and where it differs from other forms of martial arts. The information you get from this book is there to help you familiarize yourself with the discipline of Kung Fu while also preparing you for real action. When you read this book, you will gain theoretical knowledge and easy-to-apply techniques.

The volume is full of images and well-explained instructions about the different moves and stances you should know. You can easily practice each move thanks to all details provided. You will also find plenty of images that will help you get a better idea of what some of the moves and stances look like.

The book is unique in that it is specifically designed for novices and those interested in Kung Fu. All the terms are explained in a simple and easy-to-understand way. It is also up to date, and it presents comparisons to other forms of martial arts. Kung Fu continues to evolve, and this text provides you with the latest information you may need to improve your skills.

If you are looking to gain expert tips to improve your Kung Fu skills, this book is for you. It provides a hands-on approach to help beginners master different techniques. While you require a coach to train you in different elements of this martial art, with this book, you will realize that some of the other things are self-taught. More importantly, all the information is easy to understand, and you can perform some of the drills without any assistance. If you're looking for the ultimate way to start your Kung Fu journey, this book is your best option.

Here's another book by Clint Sharp that you might like

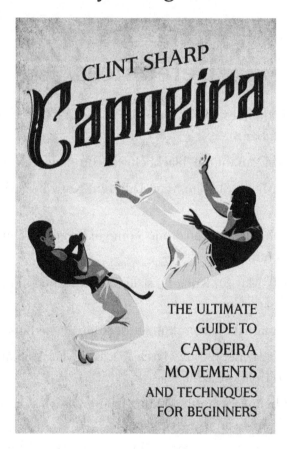

References

Kung Fu - techniques, kicks, forms (taolu), etc. - black belt wiki. (2018, September 8).

Blackbeltwiki.Com. https://blackbeltwiki.com/kung-fu

Li, S. (2019, March 6). The Main Different Kung Fu Styles. China Educational Tours.

https://www.chinaeducationaltours.com/guide/culture-chinese-kungfu-styles.htm

Robert. (2020, May 3). Kung Fu styles are explained in detail. Wayofmartialarts.Com.

https://wayofmartialarts.com/kung-fu-styles-explained-in-detail

Black Belt Magazine. (2011, March 21). Kung Fu Animal Style #3: Crane. Black Belt Magazine.

https://blackbeltmag.com/the-5-kung-fu-animal-styles-of-the-chinese-martial-arts/kung-fu-animal-style-3-crane

Leonard Lackinger, S. W. W. (n.d.). The Five Animals of Shaolin Kung Fu - Part 1. Shaolin-Wahnam-Wien.At. Retrieved from

https://www.shaolin-wahnam-wien.at/kungfu-5-tiere-1-en.php

martial. (2018, February 13). Kung Fu Animal Styles.

Martialtribes.Com.https://www.martialtribes.com/kung-fu-animal-styles

Tai Chi vs. Tae Kwon Do. (2010, December 9). Sportsrec.Com. https://www.sportsrec.com/329232-tai-chi-vs-tae-kwon-do.html

The Five Shaolin Animals. (n.d.). Kungfuforlife.Ca. Retrieved from https://www.kungfuforlife.ca/the-five-shaolin-animals.html

(N.d.). Laugar-Kungfu.Com. Retrieved from https://www.laugar-kungfu.com/style-5-animals

Shaolin Kung Fu Stances – Spirit Dragon Institute. (n.d.). Spiritdragoninstitute.Com. Retrieved

from http://spiritdragoninstitute.com/kung-fu/shaolin-kung-fu-stances

The Basic kung fu Stances / Horse stance /Taizu kung fu Camp. (2021, January 20). Learnshaolinkungfu.Com. https://www.learnshaolinkungfu.com/kung-fu-stances

5 KUNG FU STANCES (step by step tutorial)

Crane Stance. (n.d.). I-Budo.Com. Retrieved from

http://www.i-budo.com/techniques/basics/stances/crane-stance

Korahais, S. A. (2012, September 26). History of qigong: The 18 Luohan hands.

Flowingzen.Com. https://flowingzen.com/4862/18-luohan-hands-qigong

Lohan Qigong 18 hands system and history. (2018, July 27). Taichimontreal.Com.

https://taichimontreal.com/chi-kung/lohan-qigong-system

Shaolin Eighteen Lohan Hands. (n.d.). Shaolin.Org. Retrieved from https://shaolin.org/chikung/lohan.html

5 tips for finding Zen in the chaos of everyday life. (n.d.). Retrieved from Lovehemp.com

website: https://lovehemp.com/blogs/news/5-tips-for-finding-zen-in-the-chaos-of-everyday-life

8 powerful ancient qigong exercises for cultivating healing energy in the body. (2016, January 19). Retrieved from Consciouslifestylemag.com website:

https://www.consciouslifestylemag.com/qigong-exercises-healing-energy

Bailey, P. (2020, June 29). 10 tips to find zen in the chaos of everyday life. Retrieved from

Mindbodygreen.com website: https://www.mindbodygreen.com/0-21510/10-tips-to-find-zen-in-the-chaos-of-everyday-life.html

Editors of Consumer Guide. (2007, November 19). Taoism and Chi. Retrieved from Howstuffworks.com website: https://people.howstuffworks.com/taoism-and-chi.htm

Find calm amongst the chaos of a stressful life by following these tips to achieve a Zen state of

mind. (2020, March 15). Retrieved from Healthshots.com website:

https://www.healthshots.com/mind/happiness-hacks/find-calm-amongst-the-chaos-of-a-stressful-life-by-following-these-tips-to-achieve-a-zen-state-of-mind

Forms of Qi - vital substances in Chinese medicine. (n.d.). Retrieved from Sacredlotus.com website:

https://www.sacredlotus.com/go/foundations-chinese-medicine/get/forms-of-qi-life-force

HeartMath LLC, C. (2013, August 29). Finding zen: Easy ways to cultivate more inner peace.

Retrieved from Huffpost.com website:

https://www.huffpost.com/entry/how-to-find-zen_b_3820554

McGinley, K. (2019, December 15). How to find your zen when you're at your breaking point. Retrieved from Chopra.com website:

https://chopra.com/articles/how-to-find-your-zen-when-youre-at-your-breaking-point

Naumann, S. (n.d.). A brief history of Shaolin temple. Retrieved from Tripsavvy.com website:

https://www.tripsavvy.com/brief-history-shaolin-temple-1495708

O'Brien, B. (n.d.). Zen and Martial Arts. Retrieved from Learnreligions.com website:

https://www.learnreligions.com/zen-and-martial-arts-449950

Prickril, B. (2014, January 3). How to harness the power of chi energy. Retrieved from RemedyGrove website: https://remedygrove.com/bodywork/How-to-Harness-Your-Chi-Power

Reninger, E. (n.d.). Qi (chi): The Taoist principle of life force. Retrieved from Learnreligions.com website: https://www.learnreligions.com/what-is-qi-chi-3183052

Retreat, N. Y. K., & View all posts by Nam Yang Kung Fu Retreat. (n.d.). Zen and the Art of Kung Fu. Retrieved from Kungfuretreat.com website: https://kungfuretreat.com/zen-and-the-art-of-kung-fu

Robert. (2020, August 30). What is Zen in martial arts. Retrieved from Wayofmartialarts.com website: https://wayofmartialarts.com/what-is-zen-in-martial-arts

Watts, A. (2000). What is Zen? Novato, CA: New World Library.

Temple, S. (2015, July 23). Shaolin Monk Weapons Shaolin Weapons.

Chinashaolintemple.Com. https://www.chinashaolintemple.com/shaolin-monk-weapons-shaolin-weapons

18 Weapons of Shaolin Martial Arts. (n.d.). Shaolinca.Com. Retrieved from

http://www.shaolinca.com/18weapons.html

Lama Kung-Fu's 8 Fundamentals. (n.d.). Angelfire.Com. Retrieved from

https://www.angelfire.com/ny/sanshou/eights.html

Lama (martial art). (n.d.). Fandom.Com. Retrieved from

https://gyaanipedia.fandom.com/wiki/Lama_(martial_art)

Lama Pai. (2018, September 29). Blackbeltwiki.Com. https://blackbeltwiki.com/lama-pai

Lama Pai Kung Fu striking techniques. (2016, April 23). Wordpress.Com.

https://nysanda.wordpress.com/2016/04/23/lama-pai-kung-fu-striking-techniques

(N.d.). Geocities.Ws. Retrieved from http://www.geocities.ws/Colosseum/4098/strike.html

Ben Stanley, T.-S. (2016, October 15). Kung Fu kicks. Whitedragonmartialarts.Com.

https://www.whitedragonmartialarts.com/kung-fu-kicks

Five Basic Kicks. (n.d.). Shaolin.Org. Retrieved from

https://shaolin.org/video-clips-3/intensive2006/kicks/kicks.html

Kongling, M. (2016, June 29). The characteristics of a good kick. 6Dragonskungfu.Com.

https://www.6dragonskungfu.com/the-characteristics-of-a-good-kick

Functional Wing Chun. (n.d.). Retrieved from Functionalselfdefense.org website:

http://www.functionalselfdefense.org/wing-chun

Wing Chun techniques for beginners – law of the fist. (n.d.). Retrieved from Lawofthefist.com

website: https://lawofthefist.com/wing-chun-techniques-for-beginners

Wing Chun techniques: Punch, palm strike, chop, elbow. (n.d.). Retrieved from

Wingchunlife.com website: https://www.wingchunlife.com/wing-chun-techniques-strikes.html

Kongling, M. (2019, April 1). 5 wooden dummy drills/exercises ideal for beginners. Retrieved from 6Dragonskungfu.com website: https://www.6dragonskungfu.com/5-wooden-dummy-drills-exercises-ideal-for-beginners

Kriel, F. (2016, October 31). Training at home for beginning students — tiger claw Kung Fu &

Tai chi. Retrieved from Tigerclawmartialarts.com website:

https://www.tigerclawmartialarts.com/the-tiger-life/2016/10/31/training-at-home-for-beginning-students

Made in the USA
Monee, IL
20 January 2024

52095311R00090